Self-Help for Men

Unlock Your Inner Alpha Male and Increase Your Self-Confidence, Masculinity, Mental Toughness, Assertiveness, and Self-Esteem

© Copyright 2020

The contents of this book may not be reproduced, duplicated, or transmitted without direct written permission from the author.

Under no circumstances will any legal responsibility or blame be held against the publisher for any reparation, damages, or monetary loss due to the information herein, either directly or indirectly.

Legal Notice:

This book is copyright protected. This is only for personal use. You cannot amend, distribute, sell, use, quote, or paraphrase any part of the content within this book without the consent of the author.

Disclaimer Notice:

Please note the information contained within this document is for educational and entertainment purposes only. Every attempt has been made to provide accurate, up to date, and reliable information. No warranties of any kind are expressed or implied. Readers acknowledge that the author is not engaging in the rendering of legal, financial, medical, or professional advice. The content of this book has been derived from various sources. Please consult a licensed professional before attempting any techniques outlined in this book.

By reading this document, the reader agrees that under no circumstances is the author responsible for any losses, direct or indirect, which are incurred as a result of the use of the information contained within this document, including, but not limited to, ―errors, omissions, or inaccuracies.

Contents

PART 1: SELF-CONFIDENCE FOR MEN	1
INTRODUCTION	2
SECTION 1: SELF-ESTEEM	5
SELF-ESTEEM AND WHY YOU NEED IT	6
Why You Need Self-Esteem	7
Consequences of Low Self-Esteem	8
Assessing Your Self-Esteem	8
Determining Your Self-Worth and Personality	10
Your Self-Esteem Analysis	11
OVERCOMING INSECURITIES AND SELF-DOUBT	13
Causes of Self-Doubt	14
Effects of Self-Doubt	14
Six Effective Remedies for Overcoming Self-Doubt	15
Self-Doubt Test	18
Test Analysis	19
BODY IMAGE: HOW IMPORTANT IS IT?	20
Feeling Good About Your Looks	21
How Do You Know You Have BDD?	24
EVEN MEN NEED SELF-LOVE!	27
Thirteen Habits to Practice in Order to Develop Self-Love	28
THIRTEEN SELF-ESTEEM HABITS TO PRACTICE DAILY	33

SECTION 2: SELF-CONFIDENCE 39
SELF-ESTEEM VS. SELF-CONFIDENCE 40
TEN INDICATORS OF CONFIDENCE 41
SELF-CONFIDENCE TEST 42
MAKING YOURSELF THE PRIORITY 45
FIFTEEN PROVEN WAYS TO BOOST YOUR SELF-CONFIDENCE 48
LIKE A BOSS: SIX WORKPLACE CONFIDENCE HACKS 54
THE SIX WORKPLACE SELF-CONFIDENCE HACKS 55
DATING CONFIDENCE: TWELVE IRRESISTIBLE STRATEGIES TO WIN HER OVER 60
TAMING YOUR OVERCONFIDENCE 69
TEN HABITS NECESSARY FOR TAMING OVERCONFIDENCE 71
SECTION 3: SELF-DISCIPLINE 74
SELF-DISCIPLINE AND ITS CORE VALUES 75
SIX REASONS WHY YOU NEED SELF-DISCIPLINE 76
WHY MEN LACK SELF-DISCIPLINE 78
MINDSET MATTERS: CHANGING YOUR LIMITING BELIEFS 80
THREE BAD MINDSETS THAT YOU SHOULD AVOID 81
SEVEN WAYS TO DEVELOP CONFIDENCE WITH THE RIGHT MINDSET 82
MINDSET SELF-TEST 85
MENTAL TOUGHNESS: THE ZERO F*CKS METHOD 87
SKILLS THAT DEFINE A MENTALLY TOUGH MAN 88
ROUTINE HABITS OF MENTALLY TOUGH MEN 90
FIVE SELF-DISCIPLINE HABITS FOR DAILY IMPROVEMENT 94
POWER GOALS: THINKING LONG TERM FOR SUCCESS 99
BONUS – TOP TEN TIPS TO BE A CONFIDENT MAN 104
CONCLUSION 106
SOURCES 109
PART 2: SELF-ESTEEM FOR MEN 110
INTRODUCTION 111
SECTION ONE: SELF-ESTEEM 112
CHAPTER 1: SELF-ESTEEM EXPLAINED 113

CHAPTER 2: COMMON FEARS AND INSECURITIES MEN HAVE 121

CHAPTER 3: SELF-DOUBT; IDENTIFYING AND THWARTING YOUR WORST ENEMY 127

CHAPTER 4: BODY-IMAGE ANXIETY, AND FOUR WAYS TO OVERCOME IT 133

CHAPTER 5: FIVE WAYS TO BOOST YOUR SELF-ESTEEM NOW 139

SECTION TWO: ALPHA MALE HABITS 145

CHAPTER 6: THE ALPHA MALE PROFILE 146

CHAPTER 7: WHY WOMEN PREFER ALPHAS 152

CHAPTER 8: ALPHA MALE HABIT #1: CONFIDENCE 159

CHAPTER 9: ALPHA MALE HABIT #2: PERSISTENCE 166

CHAPTER 10: ALPHA MALE HABIT # 3: FRAME 171

CHAPTER 11: ALPHA MALE HABIT # 4: PHYSICAL APPEARANCE 176

CHAPTER 12: ALPHA MALE HABIT # 5: MENTAL TOUGHNESS 181

CHAPTER 13: ALPHA MALE HABIT # 6: CHARM 187

CHAPTER 14: ALPHA MALE HABIT # 7: PURPOSE 192

CHAPTER 15: ALPHA MALE HABIT # 8: SELF-CARE 197

CHAPTER 16: SETTING ALPHA MALE GOALS 203

CONCLUSION 208

SOURCES 209

Part 1: Self-Confidence for Men

Unleash the Lion within and See How Your Mental Toughness, Self-Esteem, Mindset, Self-Discipline, and Dating Life Transforms

Introduction

It doesn't matter what your background is; you can develop self-confidence. This book contains proven strategies that will teach you how to boost your confidence, establish lifelong self-esteem, conquer self-doubt, and enhance your self-discipline. When you finish reading this book, these things will no longer hold you back. You will genuinely believe in yourself, and you will reach your full potential.

Self-confidence is a mighty force within you. It affects your success at work, with your family, and in relationships. The purpose of this book is to unpack this force and present it to you in a concise, easy to comprehend manner. It is suitable for everyone—all ages, men, women, coaches, employees, students, adolescents, and of course, you.

This book will lead you down the path of believing in yourself, which is the essential asset you need in your life. Riches and fame cannot be substitutes for a lousy self-image. Lack of confidence will always hold you back and make you under-achieve. Additionally, low self-esteem often leads to divorces, horrible parenting, relationship problems, drug abuse, unemployment, poverty, et cetera. If you are a victim of any of these, then buying this book is the wisest thing you have done for yourself. The impact of the lessons in this book, if followed religiously, are permanent and will transform your life for good. You will notice a tremendous change in your confidence in less than two months.

Unlike other related books, the strategies in this book are very practical and have been carefully structured to assist you in building your confidence, self-esteem, and self-discipline quickly. However, to benefit from this book, you will have to do more than just read it. You must do the proposed exercises in the book. For example, if you are requested to take a pen and paper to do something, you should take a pen and paper and write as advised.

Here, we will use proven methods of cognitive-behavioral therapy to increase your confidence by changing how you interpret your life. We will use easy steps to uncover and analyze negative self-statements that you probably make. We will also teach you how to create new goals in life and make positive self-statements that will foster your self-confidence—as opposed to undermining it. This book will equip you with the necessary skills to squash doubt and substitute it with confidence.

This book focuses entirely on taking action. It contains proven steps and strategies on how to identify that low self-confidence is harming you and prevents you from succeeding in life. Developing your confidence requires taking practical steps, in addition to changing your beliefs or practicing positive thinking.

Each section is divided into easy to read chapters that contain information, insight, case studies, inspiration, and strategies that guarantee a rapid transformation in your life.

Besides discussing tips that will help you to grow your self-confidence, it further discusses the various ways for you to become a mentally stronger man. This book is packed with both theoretical and practical techniques for developing your own male self-confidence.

This book can be used as a guide from which you can select techniques that best fit you. This means you can develop your self-worth without even reading the entire book. Each part of the book is summed up with concise chapters that will help you go straight to the specific issues that you are lacking and that you wish to develop or strengthen.

Investing in developing your self-confidence is like investing in your whole life, and buying this book is the first step. I'm glad you have chosen to invest in yourself. Read this book at a pace that will allow you to absorb as much content as possible. Let the fantastic journey begin!

SECTION 1: Self-Esteem

Self-Esteem and Why You Need It

In this chapter, we will unravel what self-esteem is, its causes, how to overcome low-self-esteem, and explain why self-respect is important in your life, with particular emphasis on men.

Everyone in the world has self-esteem, men and women, teens and adolescents. Each has a way that they look at themselves. For example, happy people tend to have high self-esteem. On the other hand, people facing problems or stress will likely have low self-esteem. Additionally, some people exhibit excessive self-esteem that impedes their relationships with others. You are in one or more of these categories—recognizing which ones is the first step to fixing your self-esteem problems.

Self-esteem is defined as how you value yourself; it is how you perceive your value to the world and others around you. In psychology, self-esteem is defined as a sense of self-worth and personal value. Self-worth defines your competence in managing what life throws your way and it defines what it takes to feel worthy of happiness.

There is a thin line between self-esteem and self-acceptance. Self-esteem can be looked at as being internal, while self-acceptance is more about the perception outside of yourself. Self-esteem can be developed from any number of sources, including:

- Your self-appraisal.

- Family or parental support and approval.
- Acceptance by friends, colleagues, and teachers.
- How you handle challenges that come your way.

If you have positive self-esteem, you have mastered your self-acceptance, and you feel worthwhile because you feel you are contributing positively to the world. Lasting and robust self-esteem is usually based on your inherent qualities and unique characteristics.

Why You Need Self-Esteem

Developing healthy self-esteem or self-worth will help you in many ways, including:

- When a loss or defeat happens, you will bounce back quicker and will be motivated to start anew faster.
- You will understand that falling down is inevitable, and that getting back on your feet is more important.
- It helps develop your ego, which will help you get a job, find a relationship, or pick yourself up after a failure.
- Positive self-esteem helps you to heal faster. It gives you the motivation to fight on and positively face the challenges that life throws at you.
- Positive self-esteem is the foundation of your wellness.
- Your happiness, psychological resilience, and impetus to live a productive and healthy life is dependent on your self-esteem.

Self-esteem is the belief that you are as worthwhile as anyone else. You should not confuse self-esteem with overconfidence, which can be a cause of failure in life.

In a nutshell, believing in yourself is the key to having happiness and success in your life. Self-esteem is more about how you feel about yourself as a person. Like many men, you may base your self-worth on external factors like the amount of money you make, what you own, your looks, or the number of friends you have. Unfortunately, these external factors often change, and this is bound to affect your self-esteem.

The exercises in this book will help you to grasp self-esteem from the inside, feeling competent and confident in how you handle life's challenges. It is the confidence in knowing that you can accomplish your goals and that you are contented with who you are.

Consequences of Low Self-Esteem

Conversely, low self-esteem will often lead to depression, anxiety, anger issues, personal pain, and other distressing psychological problems.

- Low self-esteem will lead you to exhibit little or no regard for yourself; you will not respect or admire yourself.
- You will show a lack of confidence in yourself and will, in turn, belittle yourself with self-limiting thoughts.

Identifying the negative effects of low self-esteem in your life is the first step in realizing that you need to make changes in your life. If you feel you have a low sense of self-worth, it is important to recognize the bad habits that prevent you from achieving your personal goals.

If you have low self-worth, you will feel like nothing matters. You will feel like you are alone, even when you are with friends. Low self-esteem will make you feel disconnected from others. It makes you think that people are taking advantage of you and that they don't see you as an important person. This often leads to withdrawal, since you will be exhausted from trying to make people appreciate you, and hence you will end up giving up on life itself. If it is not handled in time, you may reach a point where you will see no reason for waking up in the morning, because you feel no one appreciates what you do and that they don't even care.

Assessing Your Self-Esteem

When you need medication, you must present the drug store with a prescription before they give it to you. With self-esteem, you must be able to assess your current situation. In this test, you will be required to take a pen and paper and follow the instructions.

This exercise will help you understand what is lacking in your life, making it easier to find the tips in this book that will help you.

Self-Esteem Test 1

Write down the answers to these questions on a piece of paper:

1. What are the situations that cause you to feel inferior or to have a low sense of self-worth? Is it when you receive criticism? When you don't feel loved or when you are rejected? Describe the situations in detail.

2. What negative thoughts do you have? Do you often feel sad? Or inferior, or jealous? Describe here all the negative emotions that affect your self-esteem and confidence.

3. When you have a negative mindset, how do you handle that situation? Do you address yourself harshly or with self-respect? List some of the negative thoughts that affect you.

4. What is the consequence of low self-esteem? How does it affect your relationships?

5. Think of someone who you consider honorable and worthwhile. Who is this person? What makes you find him or her worthy? Describe the person in detail.

6. Do you have too much confidence? If yes, how does that differ from arrogance?

This exercise will help you to identify your self-esteem status. You will learn what affects your self-esteem; it's only when you can identify this that you can start to fix it.

Self-esteem enables you to appreciate yourself. Negative thoughts and beliefs will prevent you from reaching your potential. Cognitive therapy (CT) has been used in psychology to help men recognize and change these negative thoughts. Cognitive therapy is a well-researched methodology and is the primary treatment for depression.

Several factors can influence your thinking. For instance, the situations you experience in life can change how you think. If, for example, you have been abused sexually or repeatedly, you may think you have been treated as an object and may choose to be one. Your social environment, composed of media, friends, and family, can affect the way you think about things and the way you learn.

Although external events can influence the way you think, cognitive therapy assumes that you are individually responsible for the thoughts that you choose. You can't control how others treat or perceive you, but you can control how you think and what you think.

From the discussion above, you can see that self-esteem is a very elusive concept. You must decide what is important in your life and the steps or actions you need to take to achieve self-worth.

Determining Your Self-Worth and Personality

Do you ever ask yourself, "Who am I?" Studies have suggested that your true self-esteem is based on who you are when no one is looking at you. And the only person who can answer that question is you. True self-worth is personal, in-depth, and complicated. Psychologists have suggested that you may have multiple selves, but, more often than not, you will choose one of those selves and focus on that.

People outside may look at you as a very bright, young, and happy man. Look at yourself and ask yourself if this is an accurate depiction of who you are. The public may have the wrong perception of who you are. This is a perception that you have created by how you package yourself up and present yourself to the outside world. Internally, your private self may differ significantly from your public self. You may pretend to be something that you are not just to fit in, or at least to avoid standing out.

If you have high self-esteem, you will find a way to blend your public and private self to create a close partnership; in this way, the two can complement each other to enhance your self-worth.

In the next test, I will use the self-esteem question to determine your personality. Establish whether you have a competency-driven personality or desirability-driven personality. Or if you have the characteristics of both types. Take out a pen and paper and honestly write down the answers to the questions below:

(Indicate whether it's: "True," "False," or you are "Undecided.")

7. You feel good when you get tasks done.

8. Your self-esteem increases when you get paid well for the work you do.

9. When your personal life conflicts with your professional obligations, you usually prioritize your professional responsibilities.

10. You don't compromise on everything in your life.

11. Even though you appreciate being told that you are loved, you prefer to be considered competent at what you do.

12. When something goes wrong, your first thought is how you might have messed things up.

13. You don't cancel an income-generating task for social engagements.

14. You don't take succeeding in love lightly and always work hard to excel at what you do.

15. You usually define yourself by what you do and not by how much your friends and family like you.

16. You can comfortably achieve things on your own, including luxuries like traveling and pursuing other interests.

17. You can't handle being competitive when faced with dire situations.

18. Even though you appreciate being told that you are a good guy, you prefer to be considered smart.

Your Self-Esteem Analysis

After answering the 12 questions above, add up your "True" responses, followed by your "False" responses, and lastly, the "Undecided" responses. Write the scores on the piece of paper.

If you happened to answer "True" more than "False":

✔ It means that you base how you feel about yourself on how competent you are.

✔ You define yourself by the tasks you handle, and you care more about being capable of handling these tasks than being independent.

If you happened to answer more questions with "False" than the other two options:

✔ It means you base your feelings about yourself on your desirability.

✔ You are not concerned at all with what you do.

✔ You are keen on being liked and being seen as the right person for handling tasks.

If you have a lot of "Undecided" responses:

✔ It means you are high on both competency and desirability.

✔ You prefer being competent and liked at the same time.

✔ You are likely to be stressed, since both performance and interpersonal issues will cause you to doubt yourself.

Therefore, this test shows that self-esteem is a combination of self-confidence and self-respect. Your need for self-esteem is your need to know that the choices that you make are appropriate to your life and well-being. Since you must select your goals and actions, your sense of efficacy and security requires the belief that you are right in your method of choosing and making decisions. Self-confidence, on the other hand, is how reliant you are on your mind as a cognitive tool. It doesn't mean that you cannot make mistakes; it is instead the belief that you can think and judge correctly.

Overcoming Insecurities and Self-Doubt

Self-doubt is a feeling that you have about your own abilities or actions. This means that self-doubt is not just about your present feelings, but it correlates with your past. This may cause you to say, "I have never been good at doing this and that, so why should I bother trying today?"

Self-doubt is a critical aspect of life, but when you have it in excess, it will drastically affect your confidence and will interfere with your ability to set and work toward your key objectives. Self-doubt will affect all aspects of your life, from your job to your leisure time and home activities, to relationships. Personal insecurities constrain affirmative action and cause distress, misery, and avoidance.

Coupled with fear—especially the fear of failure—self-doubt has the same effect that you might get when you try something new; for example, going on a first date, learning to swim, sky diving, or even skiing.

Self-doubt can make you become your own worst enemy. Being insecure will entirely crush your confidence. Men rarely attribute inadequacy to self-doubt, but your mood, action, arousal, and motivation are all directly affected by your sense of security. A financially insecure man will exhibit low self-esteem and a lack of confidence.

Doubt may cause you to underachieve and work below your real potential. Insecurities will make you feel that you are not prepared or skilled enough to handle a particular task—when, in the real sense, you are well equipped to handle the challenges before you.

This section will help you to recognize doubt and understand how it shapes your perspective of the world and, consequently, your feelings and responses.

Causes of Self-Doubt

There are many events that may occur in your life that will lead you to doubt yourself or your capabilities. But the most prevalent causes of self-doubt or insecurities include:

- People looking down on you – this often happens when your friends or family ignore you or undermine your contribution in the activities that you think they should have consulted you on. Sometimes friends will give up on you; they may say that you are not good enough for the task at hand.
- Under-achievement – this occurs when you perform below the required standards. It may lead you to doubt your ability to accomplish critical tasks.
- Historical failures – past failures will make you fear certain activities that you believe you will fail at just because you did not succeed in the past.
- Unaccomplished objectives – you may fail to achieve your goals; discouraged because of fear, or if you have failed in the past and think that you should not try again.

Effects of Self-Doubt

Self-doubt will negatively affect your performance and, at the same time, limit you from attaining your set objectives. Self-doubt will lead to:

- Little or no drive to achieve your goals.

- It will limit your success in life. Succeeding in life requires confidence and the belief that you can handle the challenges presented to you at any time.
- Self-doubt will lead you to have little or no sense of fulfillment. To lead a fulfilling life, you need confidence in yourself and the satisfaction that your friends and relatives have confidence in your abilities.

As highlighted in the above discussion, insecurities and self-doubts constitute a significant concern, and they inhibit your ability to face challenges in life and to reach your peak performance. Thus, it is necessary to find effective ways of overcoming self-doubt. Now it begs the question, how should you overcome self-doubt and insecurities?

Six Effective Remedies for Overcoming Self-Doubt

To conquer self-doubt, you should develop habits that will push you to see the big picture and that you are in control of your life. There are several ways to overcome self-doubt, and you will find below a discussion of six effective means of curing self-doubt:

1. **Acknowledge your capabilities.** You are not supposed to always play it safe and chase the low hanging fruits. You should push yourself to achieve more than you think you can handle. From childhood, you are trained to follow specific norms and to believe realistically. But this approach can, at the same time, be limiting; it will discourage you from tackling new challenges.

2. **Disregard negative voices within you.** The adage "hear no evil" makes sense here. When you close your ears to negative voices, you will achieve more and exceed expectations. Negative views will affect your motivation to achieve your goals. Society may send negative signals to you. For example, it can sway you to quit pursuing a particular goal. These negative voices should "fall on deaf ears" for you to achieve your objectives without limiting thoughts. You should

stand up for what you think is right. Stick by your goals and desires. If you do this, you are more likely to retire a happy man because you will not regret what you have not done in the past. You will have little or no "unfinished business."

3. Have your support group. Take the example of Nick Vujicic. Vujicic was born without arms and legs and is considered a warrior when it comes to confidence and self-doubt. He has beaten all odds by doing just about everything—from swimming, to cooking and dancing, among others. Nick Vujicic does everything an average human being does. He currently motivates people through his organization called "Life Without Limbs."

Nick Vujicic motivates fellow men and women who are born with the same condition. To achieve all these things, he has received great help and assistance from his support group. These are the people who encourage and help him to soldier on in life. They can be friends, family, sponsors, organizations, and societies that believe that his cause to transform people is worthy. Nick Vujicic's parents never gave up on him. His parents encouraged him to try everything, because they thought that he would never know what he can and cannot do if he doesn't try it out.

With that positive affirmation and support from his parents, Vujicic learned how to fish, swim, snowboard, bath, and live independently. Vujicic was determined not to be a burden to anybody, even his wife, Kanae. Vujicic's wife, Kanae, gives excellent support to him through thick and thin. They now have a lovely family together.

Men often need a support group to uplift their spirits every day. These are the people that care about you, and they will make you feel better when things go south. The advice and counsel of such people matters a lot in your decisions and, as a result, directly affects your confidence and self-esteem.

4. Be modest and always willing to learn. Ego can cause you to either underachieve or over-achieve. It is the ego that keeps you in check. As Newton's third law of motion states: for every action, there is always an equal and opposite reaction. Therefore, an overinflated ego may seem fine at first. You may have fun showing off, bragging, and looking down upon your peers. But when situations change and you fail in one thing or the other, the experience will be very traumatizing. You will crash and may take longer to recover.

It is because of this that you are encouraged to have humility of the highest order. Being humble is closely related to self-doubt. Humility is a trait that is welcomed by many people. It is the trait that will help you to calmly make decisions during the highs and lows of life. You will only succeed in life if you put your overall objectives above the desire to be recognized.

Besides, you should have a thirst for knowledge. You should be willing to learn new things. As a result, you will end up doing many things, and these successes will help grow your self-confidence. At any time in this life, provided you are healthy, there will be more to learn and even much more to improve.

5. Strive to beat your record daily. If you are successful, you will always strive to beat your previous achievements, as opposed to beating other people. It is detrimental to compare yourself to other people. In life, our destinies and efforts vary greatly. You have your own time to succeed, your own goals, and your own view of life.

Some people will be lucky. Luck is a huge factor that is often underestimated by many. But humans fail in many ways. You may meet the wrong person or partner in life, leading them with you on the path to failure. The road to success is unique for every human being. You cannot copy another person's success and make it yours. It doesn't work that way.

It is crucial to evaluate your capabilities and set practical goals for yourself. This is because, if you strive to become the next Bill Gates, your journey will be marred with self-doubt because your goal is not realistic, and you will eventually be disappointed.

6. Always work hard. The reality of life is that not everybody will be talented enough or will have the ability to succeed in a specific field. But once you accept this about yourself, you can then have confidence, patience, and perseverance to assist you in your achievements.

Working hard entails putting in some more effort continuously with the end goal in mind. By so doing, you will be insulating yourself from self-doubt because you will always have the desire to keep trying constantly. Just like Thomas Edison once said, we should not call it a failure, but instead, it's just 10,000 ways that won't work. Keep working hard, and remember that the shortcomings in the world outweigh the successes. Only if you have the willpower to move past your failures will you be successful. You should not allow room in your mind for self-doubt. Always be determined to climb, without letting negative voices or other people bring you down.

Self-Doubt Test

When you are about to face a challenge in life, and you think your self-doubt and insecurities may pull you down, it is important to take a self-doubt test that will help you to identify the areas where you should be vigilant. You will need a pen and paper to do this test. This is a simple "Yes" or "No" test that will help you discover what is limiting your capabilities. Tick either "Yes" or "No":

Imagine you were offered a job at your dream company. You have been struggling for years to get this chance, and now it has presented itself. Take this test on what you imagine is the day of the interview or appointment. You can also take this test before a real job interview, or new job.

- Do you have the necessary skills to do this job?
_ Yes _ No
- Did your previous employment prepare you for this new job?
_ Yes _ No
- You grasp new concepts fast.
_ Yes _ No
- You always ask questions when you need help.
_ Yes _ No

- When faced with a challenge, you always soldier through.
_ Yes _ No
- You are calm even in tense situations.
_ Yes _ No
- You can handle this job.
_ Yes _ No

Test Analysis

How many questions did you answer "Yes" to above? If your answer to at least five questions was "Yes," then you are in the best state of mind to face the job. It means you are capable of handling the job responsibilities. Thus, you should not doubt your capability to handle the task at hand. Go with a straight mind that you will shine at the job.

If you answered "Yes" to less than five questions, then it means you have some self-doubt. It means you doubt your ability to handle the tasks that the job requires you to handle. Self-doubt usually leads you to ask yourself unrealistic questions and may hinder you from achieving what you are skilled to achieve. Here, you should try re-affirming yourself, because if this is your area of expertise, you must be able to handle the situation at hand.

From the above test, we can see that there is a thin line between realistic concerns and self-doubt. It means you may stress yourself and look down on yourself—simply because you doubt yourself. Identifying this self-doubt is the first step in your journey to success.

Body Image: How Important Is It?

What do you think about your body image? Do you like it? Would you wish it was in some way different? If so, then you aren't alone: many people don't like the way their body is structured.

Most likely, you have looked at yourself in the mirror and thought that you look fat, or too thin. You have emphasized the flaws on your face, thinking the nose is too large, lips are too small or too big, and so on. These negative affirmations put yourself down. Men always look at their shoulders and think they are not broad enough, or that their stomach is bulging, or they believe that they are not manly enough. Men are just as concerned about looks as women are. Body image is something that every human being has to contend with.

Your body image is your natural look. It comprises of how you look, weigh, whether you are tall, short, et cetera. Your self-worth will affect the way you see your own body and how you deal with body image matters. When you have low self-esteem, it means you look at your body in a negative light. When you look at yourself in the mirror every day, all you see are flaws, and you will often point out everything you think is wrong with your body.

This may lead you to ignore things that you can do to make yourself look better, like eating healthy, exercising regularly, and dressing up. Low self-worth can make you hate your body, and you may end up not looking at yourself in the mirror.

Looking down on yourself and how your body looks like may lead you to destructive habits like starving yourself, anorexia, binge eating, and sometimes bulimia. Such practices can be life-threatening if not treated in time. And as you get older, the changes in your body become even more challenging.

From the explanation above, you will notice that body image has a lot to do with how you relate to your body. It is your relationship with your body, how you think about yourself, feel about yourself, and your view of what good looking is. In this section, we will explore how you relate to your body and how important this is to your self-worth. It is possible to look at yourself in a positive light and to love your body image.

Your body image is how you see yourself in your mind. As a man, you may often underestimate your body size and masculinity. If you are dissatisfied with your body image, it will make you unhappy for your entire life. Changing your body image can be a frustrating and disappointing endeavor.

Remember, feeling good about how you look has a lot to do with things other than just your weight and body shape. Men are always concerned about their looks, although there is the perception that women are more vocal about their looks and invest a significant amount of time and money in enhancing their looks at any given time. This book will look at body image in a broader sense. The journey toward accepting how you look can be challenging. But this section will explore the strategies necessary to improve your self-confidence by first accepting your body image, how you look, and how you wish others to perceive you.

Feeling Good About Your Looks

Let's use an example of "Paul"—for this, you are Paul. You are a smart and attractive lawyer. You have achieved a lot in your life and your workmates like you. But you are always alone at home when it comes to attending parties and movie nights. When asked, you may say that you have been too busy to socialize lately. But the truth of the matter remains that you are afraid to meet new people; and worse still, you are scared of meeting and talking to ladies.

You have a receding hairline that makes you think that no one will like you that way. You usually avoid asking ladies out unless pushed by friends. Even when you are on a date, you do not concentrate on the conversation because you are always thinking that the lady is looking at your hair. You look at the receding hairline as balding, a unique feature that your peers don't have. Your self-doubt creeps into your job, and you start missing appointments with colleagues.

With this example, we see body image as an inner personal view of your outer body. It is how you perceive your own body and your overall appearance. How you appear for real has little relation to your sense of attractiveness. When a man is handsome, this doesn't guarantee the right body image. You can be beautiful but still be dissatisfied with your looks. You can be told several times that you look good, but you see yourself in an entirely different light.

Why Do You Look at Yourself Differently?

Body image has a lot to do with how you see yourself. A poor body image will focus on the parts of the body that you hate, and forget the ones that you find attractive. Consequently, you may have a distorted view of yourself. You may be preoccupied and worry about your skin tone, and never pay any attention to your own attractive smile, a feature that people see quickly the first time you meet.

Your body image will affect how you:
1. Think;
2. Feel; and
3. Act.

A negative body image will make you feel dissatisfied about yourself, and you will end up wasting time being preoccupied with yourself. It can make you feel inadequate and frustrated. On the contrary, the right body image makes you more self-confident, increases your self-esteem, and you end up liking yourself more.

An adverse body image will make you beat yourself up for your small flaws. It makes you monitor your environment keenly for clues that relate to your appearance. This makes you very sensitive when people are around you, and more so when someone comments on your looks. This will cause you to be very insecure, anxious in social setups, and you will avoid some things, since they make you feel uncomfortable. It makes you feel less masculine, which will, in turn, reduce your sexual pleasure, and that can lead to also hurting your self-confidence.

A negative body image makes you feel that you are a less desirable person, and will make you feel discouraged about your future. This may sometimes even cause you to stay the whole day indoors, since you don't want people to look at you. It may cause you to compare yourself with people that you consider more attractive and thus will make you spend a lot of time and effort trying to improve your looks. This habit, feeling, and behavior will cause you to fail or feel inferior. The more you feel dissatisfied with your looks, the longer that feeling will stay, and thus the more you are likely to suffer as a result.

To handle a negative body image, consider that you are not alone in this world. Yes, you are uniquely made, but it doesn't mean no other people are sharing your peculiar features. Many people are dissatisfied with how they look. This often increases at some stage in life like puberty and teenage age or middle age. At this stage, you may become sensitive to how your hair, skin, and even clothing looks.

What Is a Natural Look?

If you are concerned about how you look, you are better off trying to eliminate some concern about normality and instead examine how the same concerns are impacting your own life. Being discontented with your appearance should be handled carefully, as it can end up severely affecting you. Thinking about looks can affect your whole day, leaving you attached to the mirror and concerned that you don't look right.

The critical factor here is how preoccupied you are with how you look and how it is affecting your life. There is a thin line between having a healthy and unhealthy outlook, especially in a society that is full of people who are not satisfied with how they look.

It's tough to decide whether distress and impairment as a result of doubts about appearance should be considered normal, or should be categorized as a psychiatric sickness. Severe worries about looks is a sign of some mental disorders too. Therefore, Body Dysmorphic Disorder (BDD) needs to be diagnosed by a specialist who comprehends the differences. If you have anorexia nervosa, for instance, you are always concerned about how you look, but anorexia is often associated with harshly disturbed eating habits, and the preoccupation with appearance focuses entirely on weight.

Symptoms of BDD often resemble other disorders, which can easily cause misdiagnosis and the wrong treatment to be delivered.

BDD usually begins during adolescence. It becomes chronic, even lasting longer without improvement. BDD is more prevalent in men as compared to women.

How Do You Know You Have BDD?

It is crucial to have an idea of how severe your issue is before you address it. Therefore, the test below may give you clues as to whether you have BDD or not. This diagnosis can only be made by a qualified professional, however. This book will only offer you guidance on how to identify the signs and symptoms of BDD.

In case you answer "Yes" to all of the questions, your problem is not related to bad eating habits; instead, you may be suffering from BDD. When your BDD is extremely distressing or impairing, you should visit a clinician. Similarly, if you doubt your ability to use self-help, consider engaging a qualified psychiatrist with experience in handling BDD. This is a sensitive disorder and often mishandled by people who don't have a clear idea of how it should be treated.

Signs of BDD
Answer the following questions honestly. These questions will give clues as to whether you are affected by BDD or not.
1. Do you hate the way you look?
2. Do you think about how you look for more than three hours daily?
3. Do you consider your worries about your looks as being excessive, or have people told you that you look beautiful or handsome and that you worry too much about how you look?
4. Do you involve yourself in activities with the intention of hiding, or fixing your looks? For instance, looking at the mirror, comparing yourself with other people, and excessive grooming behaviors.
5. Do you avoid places, people, or activities just because of your looks? For instance, do you keep out of bright lights or avoid mirrors, dates, or huge parties?
6. Do your looks-related thoughts or habits make you anxious, sad, or ashamed of yourself?
7. Do you have difficulties with your work, school, neighbors, family, or friends because of your concerns about your looks?

Depression as a Sign of BDD
Everyone feels down sometimes, that is normal. But in case your depression lasts longer and causes distress, you may have a problem that needs urgent action. If you suspect that you are suffering from depression, take a look at these symptoms:
• Always feeling down, unhappy, and short-tempered: for many weeks, sometimes longer.
• Reduced desire to engage in your hobbies and leisure activities.
• Feeling tired and have low energy, in spite of lack of activity.
• Increased or reduced appetite, with noteworthy weight gain or loss.
• Trouble sleeping, waking up too early in the morning or sleeping more than usual.

- Feeling slowed down, restless or fidgety, diminished ability to make decisions or difficulty concentrating.
- Feeling worthless, guilty, or hopeless.
- Excessive thoughts of suicide or death.

Over 75% of people with BDD show signs of depression. Therefore, if you have been diagnosed with BDD or you think you have it, and you are also experiencing some of the above symptoms, seek the help of a professional.

Even Men Need Self-Love!

It has often been misinterpreted that only women should have an excessive love for themselves. This is the wrong assumption because men equally should love themselves. Men are known to be selfless and often do not care much about themselves. But recently, this is changing, and more and more men are developing self-love.

Loving yourself is a challenge that emanates from your personal feelings of inadequacy. More and more men should be challenged to love themselves as a way of empowering them to confront the negative thoughts that they often harbor. Once the negative thoughts have been handled, you will usually start shifting to a positive experience with your entire mind and body.

When you have a limiting belief or negative attitude toward yourself, you will always be weighed down by your negativity. Once you treat yourself with love, respect, and self-care, you will genuinely grow and shine, treating others the same.

We have all learned that loving other people is a good thing, and we forget to love ourselves, although loving oneself has never been considered as a big issue. But why is this?

It may be an assumption that you automatically love yourself. Hence the only love you are supposed to work on is your love for others. By so doing, the things that affect individuals like stress and depression will not be addressed in time.

Many men don't know how to practice self-love. And you may even offensively and inappropriately equate self-love to being "gay" or "a sissy." But self-love is as important to men as it is for women. To develop self-love, you should form habits; positive habits that will boost your self-worth. In this section, we will discuss the habits that you should develop to practice self-love. There are many ways to practice self-love for men, but we will focus on the thirteen most important habits.

Thirteen Habits to Practice in Order to Develop Self-Love

1. Take a picture of yourself and keep it in your phone.

Men often consider taking "selfies" as being feminine. To increase your self-worth, it is essential to look at yourself repeatedly and affirm yourself. There is a lot of pressure in the world to look good. How many pictures do you take of yourself and then delete before you post what you consider the perfect shot to social media?

You should believe that you always look good, and affirm yourself irrespective of what you consider as a flaw. Therefore, take a photo of yourself, no matter how rugged you look, look at it, and let it stay strategically on your phone. If you like it so much, go ahead and share it on social media of your choice. This action will increase your self-love tenfold.

You can also do a mini photoshoot with a friend or family member. This will let the model in you out. Be stupid and sultry sometimes. Let yourself be free and be the star for a moment, realize that you can express yourself in any way you wish in this world.

2. Look at yourself in the mirror and appreciate what you like about yourself.

This workout can be challenging to achieve because your instinct will be to first pick the negatives about yourself. You need to push that negative voice away, even if it's only briefly. Practice doing this daily to allow positive thoughts to prevail; try positive affirmations and saying things like: "My nose looks great." Try to find the positives, and you'll eventually have a different perspective on everything.

3. Make a list of what you love in others.

If you work hard and make other people happy, you will automatically be loved back by society, family, and friends. This will increase your self-worth and, in turn, make you love yourself more and more. Such achievement is bound to boost your self-confidence and feelings of self-worth. When other people appreciate what you do for them, you will feel that you are worthy of being in the world and that you are contributing to a worthy cause. Think about the attributes you love in the people around you, and celebrate those, making them feel valued and appreciated.

When you practice doing this often, you will be a people magnet, and the entire community will appreciate you and will wish to hang around you or copy what you are doing. Thus, when you love yourself, others will automatically understand it and love you back even more. Regularly practicing this will help you to figure out the kind of person that you would like to be.

4. Read a book or a poem.

Reading is an intimate connection to the thoughts, likes, and subjects that the author loves. When you practice reading self-help books regularly, it will help to boost your self-worth. Poetry has the power to make people feel special. Love poems can be soothing or sad. Sometimes, poems will be flowery and very beautiful, and at times they will be straight to the point. Poems do open people up to love. Reading a poem or a romantic book is equivalent to falling in love and being in the author's world, and reading can give you new perspectives on life and help you to "step into someone else's shoes," which can develop compassion for yourself and others.

5. Love yourself – hug yourself and tell yourself that you love yourself.

When you love yourself, other people will love you. The world will resonate around you in the frequency that you set yourself. If you are positive about yourself and your peers, family, and friends, the world will respond with positivity too. Hugging yourself may seem silly. But that little moment will increase your self-worth tenfold. Never be afraid of showing yourself affection. When you love yourself, you will remember that you should also treat others the way you would treat yourself. That is with honesty and care. When you dearly love yourself, you open windows for yourself to love others.

6. Keep a diary of your recent achievements.

Here, you should develop the habit of recording or documenting your accomplishments. For example, take a pen and paper and write what you accomplished in the last day, followed by week, then the entire previous month. Record your achievements on the paper. Sometimes this can motivate you, but sometimes it may leave you feeling worthless, especially if you underachieved in the past. When you do this, you will be able to organize your pending tasks and know how far behind schedule you may have been. The bottom line is, when you diarize events, it helps you to plan better for the future.

7. Run away from negativity.

Negative thoughts are brought about by what we regularly feed our minds. If you continuously feed your brain with limiting beliefs, it will become part of you, and it will manifest in your poor performance and reduced self-confidence, since your ego will already have been punctured. Harmful gadgets and pieces of technology should also be avoided to nurture positive thinking. You should unfollow and exit blogs and social media sites that don't add value to your life. You should spend your time on important things. Join social media sites and websites that applaud their members and uplift them rather than weighing them down.

8. Declutter your life.

Go through your wardrobe and give away everything that you don't require. By so doing, your self-worth will increase. This is because you will develop an inner feeling of having achieved something, like helping a needy person. You may have developed the habit of keeping stuff in your house, things that you rarely use. This is like carrying a dead weight that is not necessary, a burden that can be offloaded, and you will still function well. All this means is that you should reduce the dead weight and leave only clothes that fit you perfectly and are still in good condition.

9. **Surround yourself with positive people.**

This can be a challenge that you are likely to find difficult. It is very sensitive, and the chances are that someone's feelings will be hurt in the process. And you are not an exception, since the injured feelings can be yours. Ultimately, though, this will have a significant positive impact on your life. It is quite easy to stick around with friends who pull you down, brush you off, and leave your ego hurt in the process. This is not easy for your mental well-being or self-image. You should surround yourself with people who will raise you and you can ascend to new heights together.

Of course, this is easier said than done. It's challenging to end friendships, mainly when they date back. It is essential to talk to the friends to give them a chance to understand their behavior and to change, before cutting them off. You can even go up a notch and write a letter if you are uncomfortable talking to them face to face. Ensure they know how their behavior or lifestyle derails you. People often don't understand that their comments can be hurting or wrecking you. If they try changing, you will have strengthened your friendship in turn. On the other hand, if they refuse to change for the better, you will consider yourself to have achieved what you set out to, since you spoke your mind from the outset and now you can let go of the negative friendship.

10. **Learn something new every day.**

In the past, you were young, and the entire world looked new. You can re-live the past by harnessing thoughts that build your brain. Every so often, you should allow yourself to read either a book, blog, periodical, journal, or article. You should spend some time learning something new from these books or physically as well. Try something out of your zone, like designing a website, or playing golf. Try learning how to play the guitar gradually from the basic chords to complicated notes.

11. Treat yourself.

You should consider treating yourself by taking yourself out for dinner and walks. Treat yourself to your favorite movie. You can choose a film from your childhood and watch it to enjoy it. Let yourself relax for a while and revisit the favorite parts of your past. From this, you can derive lessons that you will use in your future endeavors.

12. Practice self-talk.

Weird as it may seem, self-talk is critical when you wish to address issues about yourself. You need to interrogate yourself seriously. As discussed under body image in the previous section, you may be having problems with how a specific part of your body looks. Have a talk with this part of the body and about it at the same time. Self-talk should always be positive. Talk to yourself now and then, and by so doing, the negative thoughts will be blocked from your mind.

13. Practice forgiving yourself.

Everybody makes mistakes. But you still like blaming yourself over small errors that you have committed. Think of the transformation that you wish to witness in the long run. Then forgive yourself. Appreciate what has occurred but remind yourself that those are bygones and deal with the emerging consequences.

Significant growth in yourself will be achieved when you forgive yourself. It is easy to keep asking yourself the question "What if?" which will make you stagnate. You cannot move forward in that manner. Forgiving yourself means that you appreciate yourself as a human and that you accept you are imperfect and flawed as all humans are.

The above thirteen habits are just a few of the practices that, if done repeatedly, will enable you to love yourself.

Thirteen Self-Esteem Habits to Practice Daily

This section will give you thirteen simple, easy to implement, habits that will uplift you and increase your positive self-esteem. Committing to practicing these habits will wisely utilize your time and, in turn, will improve your life.

It doesn't take long to develop your self-esteem. There are myriad things that you can do to improve your self-worth and enhance your life. The thirteen habits detailed below have been carefully selected among many. The practices are short and to the point:

1. Choose and become proficient at something you love.

Establish a skill doing something that you love. It will require hard work and dedication to achieve this, but at the end of it, it will be worth the effort you put into it. To achieve this, you must be willing to stick to it and be determined to succeed.

To enjoy life, you must focus your potential on what you do well, rather than on your limitations. You must maximize your innate aptitudes and abilities. Every man has a weakness, and it will take courage for you to admit your shortcomings. But it is soothing to realize that you have your strengths and acknowledge that you have talents and personal qualities that others don't have.

There are different approaches to achieving this; you can either read books on the subject, talk to people in the field of your interest, or search the web and electronic media for information about the topic that interests you.

As the saying goes, "Practice makes perfect." To become proficient in a skill faster, you must practice it more often. While at it regularly, you will keep improving continuously to get better at that skill. As your competency in doing the activity grows, it will be a source of satisfaction and accomplishment for you.

The world is full of unsuccessful but talented men, but they lack confidence and persistence. You may feel, like them, that no matter how proficient you are at something, someone elsewhere is better than you. You shouldn't be one of them.

2. Research online, read books and articles that uplift you.

If you look down upon yourself, you can improve your self-worth by reading materials that help you look on the bright side of your life. You can adjust your life by taking control of what you consume online and from books.

Watching TV shows, movies, and commercials will reduce your self-worth and make you feel like you are not good enough. Your self-esteem may decrease if that is what consumes much of your time.

You should read material that underscores self-improvement, motivation, and other ways to raise your mood.

3. Always review your day's activities.

At the close of the day, evaluating what went well during the day can help to develop your self-worth. Get into the habit of setting aside a few minutes to discuss the events of the day with yourself. The right way of approaching this is by closing your eyes and relaxing. With your eyes closed, try to go through the events of the day. Start with the morning, then midday, until you have evaluated the events of that evening. Evaluate the events that occurred, people you interacted with, and, most importantly, the decisions you made, including successes and failures of the day.

You should be thankful for all that went well during the day. To improve your self-worth, identify at least four things that you achieved successfully; always be grateful for the things that you did well during the day. After that, note the things that you could have done differently.

This simple exercise helps you to identify the good that happens in your life and shows you how you can improve it in the future.

4. Avoid behaviors that waste your time.

Discover your bad habits, and try to avoid them. Bad habits can include watching TV, playing games, excessive Internet, et cetera. These are time-wasting habits that add nothing to your sense of self-worth. In this case, you should either completely stop these habits or reduce the time allotted to them. Use those hours to do constructive, creative, and positive things.

To identify the habits that waste your time, ask yourself the following questions:

- ✔ What excites you most?
- ✔ What do you like doing, or what can you do without being forced to do it?
- ✔ What end results do you want to achieve?

5. List all your achievements.

When you feel you have a low opinion about yourself, consider listing all your accomplishments. This small exercise will transform your focus. To do this exercise:

- ✔ Get a pen and paper or use online systems. Set a time limit for the activity; this will help you to avoid spending a lot of time on the task.
- ✔ Jot down all your achievements—both when you were young and at present.
- ✔ The list should contain achievements of whichever magnitude: big or small.
- ✔ The list should include not only what you have done for yourself, but also what you have done for others.

Once you have made the list of achievements, read through them several times, affirming yourself for the achievements listed.

6. Go out with friends.

True friends will like you for who you are and will provide companionship based on that. Going out with friends will improve your bond with them. Going out includes going to watch movies or live music, shopping, the park, bowling, dinner, parties, the gymnasium, and sports events, et cetera.

7. Teach others a skill that you have perfected.

The mere fact that you can impart knowledge of a skill that you have developed to others will increase your self-confidence. When you teach others, you become a role model for them. Teaching will help you look at yourself positively as a change maker. Here, self-confidence is having the belief that you are capable of achieving something. It means you respect yourself and you believe that you have worth, irrespective of what you make out of it.

Helping students gain more insight into a specific skill will build your students' self-confidence and self-esteem too.

8. Plan a fun-filled road trip.

Planning a trip is usually for adventure and the accompanied excitement. The planning stage of the journey will give you a sense of belonging and worth. If you are allowed by your friends and family to plan for the trip, it will boost your self-worth, because you will look at yourself as a contributor to the activity.

The planning process will include some team activities like:

✔ Talking to your colleagues or friends and family who want to join in.

✔ Making and sharing a list of the fun activities that the places you have chosen to visit offer, for instance, beaches, museums, et cetera.

✔ Considering the weather patterns of the destination, and what to take for the journey.

9. Volunteering to support a cause.

Helping others for free will always make you feel good about yourself. Volunteering helps you get connected to your peers and have pride in the cause. At the same time, volunteering gives you a chance to give back to the community.

There are many benefits of volunteering that lead to increased feelings of self-worth; these include:

✔ Helping you to build your contacts and make new friends or connections. Such connections are necessary for positive self-esteem.

✔ Enabling you to practice and perfect your social skills.

✔ Feeling good that you are implementing something that important and worthy to others.

✔ Making those that you are assisting happy, and at the same time, you will be happy when everything goes as planned.

✔ Granting you the chance to try new things.

✔ Equipping you with new transferrable skills.

When you decide to volunteer to a cause(s), you shouldn't limit yourself to one organization. It is good to volunteer for many organizations; to embrace learning opportunities, and to establish whether you connect with staff.

10. Remember that your circumstances do not define you.

Negative thoughts will always lead to low self-worth. Never allow your circumstances to determine who you are. Remember that the situation you are in is temporary.

Try distancing yourself from situations that lead you nowhere. If you are dissatisfied with events that occurred in your past, you should understand that they don't determine who you are.

11. Read and write a review of your favorite book.

To top it off, you can take a selfie photo when you finish reading a book and post it to a group of like-minded readers. Doing this will improve your self-worth, since you will appreciate yourself for finishing the book. Then post a review of the book online, either on your blog or on social media. Books are amazing. Once you develop the habit of reading empowering books, your self-esteem will automatically increase.

12. List five things or more about yourself.

As discussed earlier, list the internal things that define you. Now, here we will consider the physical things that you can do to improve your self-esteem. There are several things you can do. Therefore, you should make a list of positive things that you can achieve with minimal effort. On those days that you can't seem to love yourself, get this list out and read it over and over again.

13. Put positive messages on sticky notes on your mirror.

The mirror is one spot in the house that, come what may, you will have to visit every day. It is important to surround the mirror and the entire house with positive messages. Looking at these messages every day will help to make them permanent in your mind. The sticky notes can have motivational quotes that will help trigger something in you every time you look at them.

The thirteen habits listed above are just a few among many that can boost your self-esteem. If practiced daily, religiously, and consistently, these habits will become an innate part of you. You will not even notice how you will be accomplishing them, as the processes will be so swift and effortless.

SECTION 2: Self-Confidence

Self-Esteem Vs. Self-Confidence

In part one, we explored a lot about self-esteem. In this section, we will compare self-esteem and confidence. There is a thin line between the two. Men will always wish to be confident and have high self-esteem. You may not say it aloud, but the desire is there within you.

Self-esteem and self-confidence are composite words. They are made of two parts: "self" and esteem, "self" and confidence. The first part of these words is significant.

Confidence can be viewed in three perspectives:

• As self-assuredness—here, the definition relates to your self-confidence as your ability to perform to a certain standard.

• Belief in other peoples' abilities—here, confidence emphasizes on how you would like others to behave in a trustworthy or competent manner.

• Keeping information secret or restricted to some people—here confidence is defined as hiding information from other people.

This means that confidence is not all about feeling good inside, although feeling good is a bonus.

Confidence comes with practice and how you familiarize yourself with what you do. Below are eight signs that indicate whether you are confident enough:

✔ You will be poised and well balanced.

✔ You are breathing effortlessly.

✔ You are moving toward your objectives in life smoothly and with a sense of purpose.

✔ You are proactive rather than reactive and defensive.

✔ You respond to situations and challenges rather than reacting to them.

✔ You are sure that you can deal with whatever life throws at you, even if it is out of your control.

✔ You can afford to laugh at yourself.

✔ You believe that everything will be fine in the end, however long it takes.

This section will help you to find your inner confidence and enable you to take the first step in your journey to success, however scary or hard it may seem at the moment.

Ten Indicators of Confidence

Below are ten signs of a confident man. When you act with confidence, you are likely to have some of these ten qualities:

1. Self-direction and value. If you are a confident man, you will know what you want and where you are heading and what is important to you.

2. Motivated. Confidence leads to high motivation, and you will enjoy what you do. You may be so engaged in what you do that you cannot be distracted by anything.

3. Exhibit emotional stability. As a confident man, you are more likely to be calm and focused on how you approach people and challenges. You will be able to sense difficult emotions like anger and anxiety and will work with them instead of letting them overcome you.

4. Think positive. Confidence leads to a positive mindset. You can stay optimistic and always see the bright side of everything, including challenges and setbacks. You hold positive regard for yourself and others.

5. **Aware of yourself.** You know what you are good at, and what you can handle. You know how you look and sound to others. You acknowledge that you are a human being and that you are not perfect.

6. **Flexibility.** You adapt your behavior according to the situation at hand. You can see the bigger picture while at the same time being attentive to details. You always consider other people's views while making decisions.

7. **Eager to develop.** You enjoy stretching yourself. You treat every day as a learning experience instead of acting as if you are an expert with nothing new to learn.

8. **Healthy and energetic.** You are in touch with your body and respect it, and you have a sense that your energy is flowing freely. You can handle stressful situations without burning out.

9. **Willing to take risks.** You can take risks and act in the face of uncertainty. You will put yourself on the line even when you don't have the necessary skills and answers to the situation at hand.

10. **Has a sense of purpose.** You have a high sense of the coherence of different aspects of your life.

Self-Confidence Test

The 20-point questionnaire below is derived from the confidence indicators above. To measure your confidence level, answer all the questions by indicating whether you agree or disagree with the statements in the five-point scale provided. You should take the test as many times as you like and keep track of the development.

Once you have taken the test, keep the results in a diary and do it again in four to six months, and note the development. Completing this test will help you to discover the aspects of your life that affect your confidence. Try to answer the questions accurately so that you can correctly evaluate your level of trust and prescribe the right remedy for what is lacking. Check where applicable.

Statement	Strongly Agree	Agree	Neutral	Disagree	Strongly agree
You know what is important to you.					
You know what you need in life.					
You never hate yourself for failing.					
You can stay calm and think when things get difficult.					
All you do involves things you love doing.					
You often become fully engrossed in what you are doing.					
You are quite optimistic.					
You respect yourself and people around you.					
You know your strengths and weaknesses					
You know what others consider to be your strengths.					
You consult others where necessary, before taking action.					
You are ok with looking at the big picture and intricate details in situations.					
You enjoy taking up new challenges.					
You love looking for new opportunities and learning and growing from them.					
You look after your body image.					
You handle stress well.					
You have a positive attitude toward taking risks.					
You regularly meditate.					

You have your set mission and purpose in life.					
You are self-motivated to handle new challenges					

After checking the appropriate square on each line of the questionnaire, award yourself five points for each check under the "Strongly agree" column, four points in the "Agree" column, three points for "Neutral," two points for "Disagree," and one point in the "Strongly disagree" column.

Add the points up and analyze the results. Use the rating scale below for advice based on your score. This activity will help you to know the areas of your life that require immediate attention and the sections of this book that you should skip to read immediately.

Rating

Score: 80 – 100. This means by all standards, you are a confident person. It means you have clear priorities and hopefully pursue the life you desire.

Score: 60 – 80. You are confident in many situations. Just a few areas in your life pull you down. You have a burning desire to improve your confidence and increase your self-worth. This book will help you on your journey to trusting yourself. Look at the next part of this book to improve on these aspects.

Score: 40 – 60. You have picked the right book. The tips and tricks in this book will help you to improve this score in a couple of months if followed religiously. You are just experiencing some uncertainty in your life at the moment, and you may be wondering whether you can do anything to address the situation. You need to allow yourself some time to work on the aspects that require immediate attention, and you will be happy with your progress in a few months.

Score: 20 – 40. You have very low self-confidence, but not to worry because it doesn't have to stay that way. The fact that you have taken the test has set you on the right path to building your confidence. Even if you have scored below par in this test, you can increase your self-confidence tenfold in the next 4-6 months by following the steps and principles outlined in this book. Read this book cover to cover, and you will find excellent advice that will put you on the right path to self-worth.

Once you have finished the exercise and read the advice based on your score, look at the score and note the parts that brought down your overall rating. Read chapters related to improving those specific areas of confidence. Do the exercise some months later, and you will notice progress in your evaluation. This book is full of advice and practical guidance to help you improve all the aspects that affect your self-worth.

Go over the content to identify the areas that will help you to boost your confidence quickly. The test above is simple but very powerful in monitoring the growth of your belief in yourself. The activity will also enable you to identify your strengths and weaknesses and find how to deal with them effectively.

Making Yourself the Priority

Note that self-confidence and self-esteem are harnessed when you accept yourself. Self-love is the balance between taking yourself the way you are, while acknowledging that you deserve better and then working hard toward this. From the above explanation, you will realize that you are the priority. You should make yourself the priority, for the rest of the things to fall in place.

You are not selfish when you prioritize yourself over others. It all depends on the proportions available for sharing. For example, if an orange is cut into four pieces for the four people in the room and you pick two pieces instead of one, that is being selfish. Irrespective of this, it is essential to put yourself first. You must save some energy for yourself at all times.

You are on your own in this world. Therefore, the person with whom you will be in a relationship longer than anyone is yourself. It is when you are in a good relationship with yourself that you will manage your relationships well with other people.

Unfortunately, you have to accept that even though someone may mean well, they may inflict pain on you repeatedly without minding the effect that their action or inaction and words may cause. An ideal situation would be to be in a stable place emotionally, where someone else's actions do not affect your moods.

Therefore, personal growth is an ongoing process, and it may take longer to get to where you're less affected by people's actions. In this case, you are forced to offload those people who bring you down. Some people can be venomous and will restrict your progress so that you cannot even afford a smile. Consider a plant. If placed under harsh conditions, it will not grow and will finally wither. But when placed in the right conditions, the plant will thrive and grow into a beautiful plant. Once it has grown and established its roots and stem, it will be impossible to destroy it.

Human beings can also be toxic. A toxic person is someone who:

- Negatively evaluates all your efforts;
- Demands a lot;
- Disrespects you; and
- Doesn't support your overall objectives.

Such people may:

- Laugh at you;
- Disregard you;
- Abuse you physically;
- Manipulate; and/or
- Belittle you.

These people are often not willing to challenge their harmful actions and make necessary changes. Therefore, when you find yourself around such people who are toxic toward you, you will lose your inner peace. This may force you to transfer the pain inflicted on you to other people. Now it begs the question of whether it is selfish to think of yourself here. Isn't it selfish of them to expect you to be okay with what they do to you?

Ending a bad relationship is hard, since these people may be close to you. But it is important to let go of them, because, once you eliminate those people from your life, you allow for positivity to flow into your life. You will, in the future, have enough time and ample space for self-examination, remedial work, and development, and like the plant we discussed earlier, you will definitely be able to grow.

Fifteen Proven Ways to Boost Your Self-Confidence

Confidence emanates from within every man. A man's ideas, reflections, and thoughts will help him to build his self-confidence. Below are fifteen proven ways to boost your self-esteem and hence your confidence:

1. Be Patient

A confident person must exercise patience. If, as a confident man, you don't attain your goals on the first try, you will not look at it as a failure. You will learn from the experience and strive to do better the next time a similar situation occurs. Patience is a virtue that accompanies persistence. Look at Thomas Edison, who tried inventing the light bulb and failed over 10,000 times. When he asked about his invention, Thomas said that he didn't fail 10,000 times, but instead, he discovered 10,000 ways that didn't work. That shows persistence.

2. Love Yourself

As a man, you may think it is wrong to love yourself. You consider it as being selfish, arrogant, and unpleasant. Having this kind of attitude is wrong, since you are mistaking self-love with pride and narcissism. Narcissists don't love themselves. Instead, they are in love with themselves, which is quite different.

Failure to love yourself leads to a reduced sense of self-worth, acceptance, or belonging. Additionally, your capacity to love others is directly affected by your ability to love yourself.

3. Overcome Your Fears

Overcoming something that frightens you will make you even stronger and more self-reliant. By overcoming your worries, you will develop an efficient and practical way of dealing with the challenges that you meet in life. It doesn't have to be complicated. Deal with the stress and worries that you face in your daily life. Such an approach increases your self-confidence and sense of self-worth.

Understanding your fears is the initial step to overcoming them. You should understand what threatens you and limits you from achieving your sense of self-worth. Conversely, fear stops you from leaving your comfort zone.

4. Have a Mentor

As Joe Montana once stated, confidence is a very fragile thing. This is true. Self-worth needs nurturing and continuous effort to develop it to mature and become an innate part of a man. If you didn't build your self-esteem from your parents' influence, it's not too late. It is time you identified someone you respect in your field and ask them to be your mentor. Many people will accept the request and offer to assist you.

Mentoring should not be confused with life coaching or therapy. Mentoring is merely a process by which you become more knowledgeable and experienced in a particular field; a mentor helps you to navigate the rapids of the path, since he has taken the road himself. Having a mentor in any sector is valuable. You will develop high confidence from the satisfaction that someone is willing to talk to you and guide you as you struggle to make it in life.

5. Embrace New Ideas

Embracing new beliefs when you are trying to solve problems is what learning and building self-confidence are all about. You should believe in your resources and those of the people that you trust. If you try to do everything your way, without welcoming new and innovative ideas from others, you are bound to fail.

It is wise to get input from the people surrounding you. Even though sometimes the ideas you require will come from your head, you may end up ignoring them if you have low self-worth. Being open to your thoughts is often a challenge for many men. If you are not open to different ideas from the people around you, your self-confidence will be very low.

6. Be Dependable

Knowing that you can count on the people you love, your teammates, and yourself, means you have the tools necessary to get you through rough patches in life. Doing it alone is possible, but it will take you longer. Having others in your life who are dependable always makes things easier, since you will be confident that you don't have to do it all by yourself.

Being dependable may make you more desirable. You will soar higher when people know that they can rely on you. When you realize that you can also rely on yourself, then there is no challenge that you can't handle. Confidence emanates from knowing that you or the person you need will be there when you need them.

7. Practice Positive Thinking

You may often say negative things about yourself. When this becomes a habit, it prevents you from enjoying life, achieving your objectives, or sometimes it hampers you from finding love. One of the ways to break the habit of negative thinking is to be aware of negative thoughts. Being conscious of what is going on in your head and around you, will help you to reduce the tension.

8. Avoid Procrastination

Put all the excuses away and acknowledge that you have the capacity to complete the task on time. Many men would prefer to accomplish the task at the last minute. Procrastination is a bad habit that must be eliminated for you to develop your self-confidence. To achieve this:

✔ Start timing everything, to find out how long it takes you to do something that you have been dragging on.

✔ Just do it. If you start and work on the task at hand, you will eventually have some time later on that you can utilize in any manner.

✔ Conquer your fears—some men avoid tasks for fear of failing at implementing them. This fear is an excuse that will lead you to delay or completely ignore essential things in life.

✔ Plan your free time. Always reward yourself by giving yourself a break once you have attained your milestones. Breaks are vital; you cannot be productive for the entire day. Resting makes you sharp.

9. Respond Promptly

Responding to problems rather than reacting will save you a lot of pain. Some fear may drive you to go into reaction mode. This reaction can be triggered by anxiety. To handle situations efficiently, you must learn to respond. It takes practice to stop reacting to matters and instead respond promptly to them. You should discuss these processes with someone you trust and believe in. This way, you can help each other to avoid reactions and seek appropriate responses.

10. Exercise Your Mental Strength

Take, for example, a game of chess. Someone who has won a chess game, or succeeded at chess, has spent many hours practicing. There are many ways to exercise your mental strength. The advantage of mental exercise is that it can be done anywhere, while you are running your day to day life. But remember, this is not one solution that fits all. What works with one person may not work with another.

11. Strengthen Your Support Structure

Support structures have been in existence even before the coming of psychotherapy. It is essential to have people around you who are willing to hold your hand through the challenges that life throws at you. In case you don't have friends, family, or colleagues who offer you emotional support, you can join a group that does so. Alternatively, you can create your own support group.

You can get emotional support from such groups. The help you can get from support groups will not only build your confidence but will also set you on the pathway toward living a fruitful life.

12. Celebrate Small Achievements

You don't have to be successful to be confident. Many have proven the opposite. When you develop success in any sector of your life, it will affect all the other areas of your life. Little achievements can be anything from running a few kilometers every day. You can set realistic targets for the number of kilometers you would wish to cover in a day. Once you have achieved the small goals, you should celebrate your achievements. Your self-worth will gradually increase as you appreciate the small wins in your life.

13. Keep Fit and Healthy

A healthy man will have the confidence to accomplish any task and face any challenge that life throws at him. If you are not healthy, even surviving will become a problem. Being fit is necessary for your self-esteem and physical well-being. Fitness can be achieved easily by exercising. Being healthy and assisting others to be healthy is essential to enable you to live a fulfilling life. When you are out of shape or are unhealthy, the mere basics of life will be hard for you to achieve; hence you will suffer from low self-worth.

14. Practice Giving

Assisting others will help you to know that you are a nice person and that you can have a positive impact on society. When things are tough, giving money to a worthy cause or volunteering may seem counterproductive. Even with the pressures of life, people still find ways to give. Giving money makes you feel good about yourself, hence boosting your self-confidence. By providing a little something to someone in need, even just your time and care, you build self-respect, since you believe you have contributed to making the world a better place.

15. Avoid Critical Comments

When you say something hurtful to someone, you will end up pushing them away to the point that they will not want to connect with you ever again. Here, your emotional support structures are damaged. When you regularly criticize someone, the person to whom you are directing the criticism may just be acting along to manage your tantrums. Even if you are trying to help them, you will be turning them away. Once your advice is ignored, you will feel that you are not respected. Being ignored will not be good for your self-confidence.

To avoid this negative energy, carefully think of the words you use. Before saying them out loud, imagine how you would feel if the words were directed to you; if you get upset, so will everybody else. By interacting in a manner that does not offend others or make them feel judged or held down, they will also open-up and share their opinions.

Like a Boss: Six Workplace Confidence Hacks

Confidence is an essential component in a workplace environment. Can you imagine a workplace full of employees with low self-esteem? Would you prefer working or even seeking services from such an entity? Confidence in the workplace involves assisting people in understanding their emotions.

Smart goals and tight deadlines define a work environment. Therefore, your self-confidence will increase if you can meet the deadlines and deliver a quality job performance at the end of the day.

Napoleon Hill once stated: "What the mind can conceive and believe, it can achieve." In this section, we will discuss the workplace mindset that men should adopt. While you are trying to manifest your objectives, it is crucial to keep a high vibration.

In a work setting, feelings are often exchanged among colleagues on a like-for-like basis. Therefore, you need to master everything you have learned in the previous section of this book about self-confidence and self-esteem. However, without a doubt, your belief is pivotal as far as manifestation is concerned. This means if you don't believe in something, you will not see it occurring in your life. In this section, we will explore how our beliefs affect our workplace performance and the quality of relationships in the office.

The Six Workplace Self-Confidence Hacks

Below are six workplace confidence hacks that you must know to navigate the work environment like a boss:

Hack 1: Practice Positive Thinking in Your Job Situation

Here, positive thinking refers to the practice of choosing ideas that will empower you over those that will limit you. In the workplace, a positive mind will give you a positive life.

A positive mind is superior to a negative mind in the sense that positive thinking entails selecting the thoughts and actions that support the project rather than hampering it, and it eventually brings the best outcome irrespective of the situation.

Harboring negative thoughts like "You can't do it," will prevent you from taking necessary steps toward achieving your objectives. You will then be less likely to meet the set goals.

Positive thoughts like "You can do it," will enable you to try, therefore, increasing your chances of meeting your own goals.

A negative thought process will restrict you, while a positive one will move you closer to your goals within the workplace. When you believe that something is impossible, it will mean that the barriers to success have absorbed you completely.

You should maintain a positive attitude in the workplace. A positive attitude will give you hope and, at the same time, change your perspective. In the workplace environment, you need to find people who have succeeded in what you're doing and learn from them. Your thoughts will help you move up the ranks at your workplace—or they will pull you back. Also, acknowledge that it's never too late to transform your ideas and transform your beliefs to support rather than obstruct yourself.

Hack 2: Workplace Mentality Is Your Reality

Henry Ford once quoted that: "Whether you think you can or think you can't, you are right."

Another philosopher called Immanuel Kant said that our experiences, including sensations and our perception of objects, are representations of our mind. And that reality is only based on an individual's perception.

Your perception of the workplace is dependent on your self-beliefs. These beliefs are your truths that build your subjective realities toward workplace self-confidence. A belief, here, is the feeling of certainty toward something—your lives and jobs are based on the beliefs you acquire through your experiences.

At your job, it's necessary that your personal growth is open to the beliefs of others and that you are willing to change your beliefs if convinced that an alternative way of looking at things will provide a more accurate and empowering solution.

Hack 3: Listening to Your Subconscious Mind

Within your job environment, it is vital to engage and understand the signals coming from your subconscious mind. Your limiting beliefs are among those continually taking root in your subconscious, since they are repeatedly planted there. The subconscious mind doesn't evaluate the ideas. It slowly transforms our beliefs. This means that, if you are fearful, jealous, and power-hungry, you will always sow bad seeds in yours and other minds, which will, in turn, limit your potential in life.

Hack 4: Analyzing Your Thoughts

If you cannot change a situation, try to change your view of it. That's where your power is. Either be controlled—or be in control. Your brain is intelligent. It wants to make life easy for you and to do as little thinking as possible. (This might sound a little strange, especially if you're a chronic overthinker.) So, the brain is optimized to make subconscious decisions based on previous emotions attached to experiences. This autopilot behavior brought about by repetition enables you to move through your day without having to relearn processes, such as driving, and without having to think through all the minutiae of daily life.

However, since your subconscious mind has no awareness, it can unwittingly hold you captive to unhealthy behavior. The fact that you felt terrible every time you reacted violently to abuse you may have been subjected to, for example, should make you realize that it wasn't your conscious reaction. You were conditioned to respond like that by your past experiences, and you didn't question your response because you think you lack awareness.

How you view an event determines how you experience it. Facts are neutral, but you often give them labels. When an unfortunate event happens, pause, and observe your thoughts. By doing this, your unconscious mind will replace thought with awareness. Only once you discover your thoughts, will you choose how to respond. Meditation is a powerful tool for enhancing this skill.

In summary, instead of trying to control events that are external to you, practice controlling your mind's response to them. Controlling the mind gives you back your power and is the key to a happy life. Therefore, in a workplace environment, your ultimate objective is not to just get rid of the limiting thoughts, but to analyze them first.

Hack 5: Changing Your Limiting Beliefs

It would be good to change your beliefs faster, but this is a difficult thing to achieve. Your beliefs are engraved in your subconscious mind. When you accept a notion without question, you live with it your entire life. Some ideas will make sense to you, but they will not empower you. They will only limit your potential in life and your ability to attain your objectives.

The first step is to identify the beliefs that you wish to change. For instance, let's say that one of your core beliefs is that you cannot change your future, so you won't be able to accomplish great things.

These beliefs won't make you feel good, but if you'd tried to change them right away, you would have felt as though you were lying to yourself. After all, these beliefs were your truth. But why did you *think* they were the truth?

When you confront your limiting beliefs, you will discover that you believed what you did because someone told you. These limiting beliefs that were passed onto you by some other people should be avoided at all costs.

Hack 6: Continuous Affirmation

Never underestimate the power of affirmations. These are the positive statements that describe what your goals and objectives are in life, as if you have already achieved them. Repeating something with great conviction generates a belief in your subconscious that the statement is true.

It is common in society. You are often fed certain notions about the world, which are repeated over and over again. For instance, let's say your parents continually told you that you were shy; all that happened was this was reinforced in your mind. You may not feel shy. But, through repetition of this idea, you might start believing it. Consequently, you will grow up to be shy—here, these words become a self-fulfilling prophecy.

This should remind you of the importance of surrounding yourself with people who are feeding you with empowering thoughts. This is not to say that you should only keep friends who say good things about you. But it does mean that you should pick people who are supportive, not destructive to your life's objectives.

When you are repeatedly told that you can't do something, you will end up believing that it is true. Repeating positive affirmations is a conscious process. When you send instructions to your subconscious mind, once these beliefs are planted, your subconscious mind will do all it can to bring these ideas to life. It's like coding a program to do something for you. Once the codes are correctly done, the program will deliver its intended purpose.

Repeating positive affirmations is useful in life. You can practice saying your affirmations at a time when you are feeling okay. At this stage, they will gain momentum faster by you repeating these affirmations. This habit will change your state of mind and belief systems, and as such, your reality, completely.

Practice saying affirmations in your own words and voice like telling irrefutable facts to your friend. Care should be taken only to repeat positive statements—don't recite limiting comments. You should act in a manner suggesting that the goal has already been achieved. This way, the subconscious will believe and will respond accordingly. It is upon you to allocate more time for regularly reciting positive affirmations.

Dating Confidence: Twelve Irresistible Strategies to Win Her Over

If you have picked this book, you are probably like many men out there. You have trouble and trepidation when it comes to winning women, especially when it comes to flirting and trying to get her into bed. It's a common issue for men, and not every man is a natural when it comes to charm and seduction. But it doesn't mean you cannot succeed when it comes to winning women.

Confidence is critical when it comes to women. It is an aphrodisiac to women. Women can detect confidence, since it is what they look for in a man. Dating has become a killer of men's confidence. You may even find it hard to ask a woman out for a date. You may wonder:

✔ How do you get yourself to make that move?

✔ How do you get to look her straight in the eye and make your request?

The ability to have control over sex and your love life, in many ways, defines who you are. The ability to win ladies improves your internal happiness and self worth. When you succeed in winning women, you will reap the benefits of your masculine ambition and trust in your abilities. This will consequently boost your self-confidence.

What you need to know is how to increase your chances of success in relationships. Here are twelve strategies that can get you started, in an attempt at winning over a romantic prospect:

1. Be Committed to the Cause

Here, you should take committed action to win her over, even if the response is negative. You should keep asking women out and detach yourself from the negative outcome. Don't blame yourself or look down upon yourself when the answer is always negative after several trials. It can take you over a year to get the first date. All you need to do is to stay committed to the course and if one person isn't interested, you will eventually find a match who is right for you.

2. Know Yourself

Here, you should establish whether you are gay, bisexual, straight, or not identified at all. You must determine which side you are on and accept who you are. When you know and accept yourself, you will interact easily with others. Learning to communicate efficiently with ladies and getting them to like you will help you to achieve your objective of self-confidence. You must be the kind of person you want to attract.

3. Be Yourself

After you have known yourself and accepted yourself, you should just be yourself. Do not struggle to be someone else; it's tough to keep up an act. Never give her a wrong impression of who you are, or act in a way that you cannot maintain. Ladies will fall for you if you don't exaggerate your abilities by struggling hard to impress them instead of being real.

4. Gain Confidence Before Approaching Her

In meeting women, you will always find that those men who are confident are more successful. This has nothing to do with good luck.

Women prefer you to be a confident person, not meek and unsure of yourself. Women don't like men who stand aloof and look at them secretly. Whether it is for a one-night stand or long-term, women will not consider dating a loser.

You need the confidence to approach women. When you know how to talk to women and have the right attitude, you will start to exude self-assurance. With more confidence and plenty of practice, you will find that the techniques in this book can help you to hook up with any girl you want.

5. Keep Practicing

Always practice, practice, and practice—again and again. One of the biggest mistakes that you can make in this endeavor is to start by talking to the most beautiful woman in the room.

If you are not used to doing this, you will start doubting yourself. Hence trouble will begin here because you will be making excuses right away as to why you can't approach someone. These doubts arise because you haven't invested in talking with many women to be confident enough to approach the one that you have genuinely fallen in love with.

Therefore, like any sector in life, continuous practice will help you perfect it. You will build your confidence slowly. You will begin having conversations with women—just talking, with no expectations. This includes people you are not attracted to.

Once you practice persistently, your confidence will grow, and it will be easier to start conversations with random women. With time, you will have no problem walking across that crowded room and picking the beautiful lady who has attracted you.

6. Pick a Good Dating Location

Another great tip to help you meet the type of women that you would like, and that will make it easier to converse with them, is to choose a type of venue that makes you feel at home. Perhaps you don't like the bar or club scene, for example. This could make approaching women in these locations more difficult if you hate yelling over the music or looking like a fool on the dance floor—unless, of course, you know how to dance.

Instead of using that as an avenue for meeting women, consider classes, such as an art class or a cooking class, head to the park, a farmer's market or grocery store, a museum. Find those locations that you enjoy, and you will find that you are more comfortable and confident when it comes to approaching women and talking with them.

7. Always Keep Learning

Building your confidence is a vital initial step. You can always learn new things: being curious and open to new experiences and constant learning is key.

8. Be Humorous, Hygienic, and Always Smile

These are essential aspects for you to develop before hitting on a lady. Sure, you want to get out there and meet women who are going to be interested in you and who will want to sleep with you. However, all of the talking in the world is not going to get you anywhere if you are humorless, gruff, and hygiene-challenged. Think about it from the woman's perspective for a bit. Would you want to go home with someone who did not take care of themselves, and who was grim most of the time? Probably not.

That's why this chapter is all about working on yourself and making yourself into a better catch before you start trying to hook up with women. By taking these steps now and making some improvements in your life, you will find that it can help you to build the confidence discussed in the first chapter. You are going to be happier with who you are and what you have to offer.

You will exude confidence, and that's what so many women find attractive, whether they are looking for a one-night stand or someone with whom they can build a real relationship.

9. Upgrade Your Overall Physical Appearance

We're not talking about running out and getting plastic surgery to look like whoever the current heartthrob actor or musician is right now. It's far more straightforward than that, fortunately. You will find that even if you are an average guy, or perhaps even a somewhat less than average guy, there are plenty of things you can do that will help to change and improve your physical appearance to make you more attractive.

10. Keep Fit

Your physical fitness is a vital aspect of enhancing your confidence and consequently landing the woman of your dreams. The first step is to make sure that you are taking good care of yourself when it comes to your physical fitness. Not only is it essential for your health, but it is crucial to how women perceive you. If you are hoping to sleep with good-looking women with beautiful bodies, you can be sure they want something equivalent from the men they choose.

Whether you are overweight, flabby, or nothing but skin, bones, and a little bit of muscle, you can do better. If you have some resources, spend some money and time to shed some pounds and build muscle. You don't need to have a six-pack, and you don't need to look like a fitness model. You need to make sure you are in shape and that you look good.

For many men, the journey to fitness might be longer than it is for others. Perhaps you've neglected taking care of yourself for a while now, or maybe fitness was never necessary to you. Now is the time to start getting into great shape. You are going to feel better, and you are going to look better. When this happens, you are going to be bursting with energy and confidence.

The fitness requirements will entirely depend on the body you wish to acquire, whether you are trying to lose weight or build your muscles. Some men may be skinny and may want to add some muscles. To achieve this, you can go to the gym if you have an affordable one in your area. You can also consider hiking, swimming, walking, or running. You need not spend a lot of money getting into good shape. Calisthenics and bodyweight exercises can transform your body.

The goal of this book is not to give you a bunch of workout plans that you can use. Instead, it will teach you how to pick and choose relationships with women. Getting into shape is just one of the aspects you will have to consider.

Just make sure you follow through with the proposed exercise plan and put in the necessary time and effort required to get into shape before you begin trying to strut around a club picking up women. The better shape you are in, the easier it will be to win women.

11. Dress to Impress

In addition to getting your body into shape, you need to think about other aspects of your outward appearance. This certainly includes the clothes and shoes that you are wearing.

People say that you should never judge a book by its cover. However, it's human nature to do just that. People judge based on appearances, and there's nothing you can do about that. If you were to see an unkempt woman in ragged, dirty sweatpants, wearing an old baggy t-shirt, and with a cigarette dangling out of her mouth, you are probably not going to think she's the most attractive woman in the room.

Now, think about it from a woman's perspective. If you have holes in your clothes, ratty shoes with frayed laces, and stains on your clothes that just won't come off, why would she be interested? You can't wear your favorite Velcro sneakers everywhere, no matter how comfy they might feel. You are not a professional hobo, so don't dress like it.

Sure, if you are lounging around the house, wear whatever you want. Be comfortable. When you head out, though, whether you are heading to the gym, to work, to the store, or you are going out to a bar, movie, museum, or anywhere else, dress appropriately.

You should not spend all your money on new clothing. You probably have a few things around the house that you can wear that look good, and that make you feel great about yourself. That last bit is the most important. You want clothes that work well for you and that make you look as good as possible.

Maybe you do need to spend a bit of money getting some clothes that fit better to your body shape. This is undoubtedly true if you have been working out and getting into better shape, as mentioned. If you aren't sure exactly what you should be wearing to look good or the type of clothing that will work best for you, seek help from some friends.

If you have some friends who are women—and hopefully you do—they can provide you with some great suggestions. If you aren't sure who you should be asking, then you can always spend some time talking with people in the clothing shop. They can certainly help, but don't fall into the trap of buying shoes and clothing items that are more expensive than you need.

Now that you have started to think about your physical fitness and health, and you've started to look at your wardrobe to see what you need to buy, it's time that we talked about hygiene.

12. Work on Your Hygiene

If you are an adult who has managed to get through your awkward teenage years, you should have at least a basic grounding of cleanliness and know how important it truly is if you want to attract women. However, it does still bear repeating here because there are plenty of men—too many, in fact—out there who do not care one iota about grooming.

It doesn't matter if it's just a one-night stand or a long-term relationship. If you stink with fuzzy teeth and untamed hair, you aren't going to win women. And you should not. Take proper care of your hygiene.

Get into a routine for hygiene and stick to it. Honestly, it's straightforward, and it might amaze you how many men don't seem to care. Here are some simple yet vital grooming and hygiene tips and reminders for men.

✔ **Wear deodorant.** Wear it every damned day, and maybe add some twice a day if you need it. You want a pleasant fragrance for the deodorant and antiperspirant, but not something that is going to be overwhelming.

✔ **Wash your face.** You should wash your face twice per day. Washing helps to make sure that your face is clean and is not going to break out. Stay away from using soap, body scrubs, and body gels on the face, as these can dry and irritate the skin. Use a facial cleanser instead.

✔ **Brush your teeth.** You want to brush your teeth three times per day. Do it in the morning after breakfast, after lunch, and before you head to bed. This will keep the teeth in good shape, and it helps you to maintain a white smile. I'd recommend activated charcoal by teethwhiteningsolutions.com. Your smile is essential, as you'll see later in this section.

✔ **Floss.** Brushing is essential, but don't forget just how important it is to floss, as well. Floss at least once per day, as well as whenever you feel as though something might be stuck between your teeth. If you plan to kiss a woman, you need to make sure your teeth and breath are on point. Otherwise, it's going to be a no go.

✔ **Change your underpants.** Sure, you should change your underwear daily. But do we always do this? Are there days where you say, "That's okay" and head outside? Remember always to change your underwear after a workout. Dirty underclothes are a major turnoff to ladies.

✔ **Wash your clothes.** Just because you sniff your shirts or pants and don't think they stink, and you don't see any stains, does not mean they are clean. Get into the habit of washing your clothes regularly and hang and fold them properly so that they do not get any wrinkles.

✔ **Shower at least once or twice a day.** You should ideally shower in the morning before you head out, as well as at night after a long day. Wash once a day at the very least. Besides, make sure that you shower after you have been working out. It's better for your skin, and it ensures you don't have any leftover funk on you after the gym. If you are going to be going out where you could meet someone—which is just about anywhere—make sure you are clean and fresh before you leave the house.

✔ **Clip your nails.** Take a look at your fingernails and then your toenails. Having trimmed nails is something that women often look for when they are talking to a man that piques their interest. If the nails are long enough to hold dirt, then they are too long. If the toenails are starting to curl over at the edges, then they are far too long. No, this doesn't mean that you need to invest in a manicure or pedicure. It just means you need to take a minute each day to check your nails and make sure they aren't out of hand.

✔ **Shave or trim the beard.** Having facial hair is okay, provided you keep it groomed and trimmed properly. Use beard oil and other products to make sure it is in good shape, and to make sure it doesn't stink. Yes, some men have bushy beards that stink, and that's going to be a big turn off for most women. When it comes to having facial hair, something else that you will want to remember is that not all women like it. By having a beard or a mustache, you are limiting the number of women who may immediately find you attractive. Think about whether you need a beard or not.

✔ **Groom below the neck and the belt.** you should keep in mind that you want to groom your entire body, including where she can't see when you first meet. You must consider grooming the pubic area when you do find a woman to sleep with.

The simple tips above will help you stand out above many men.

Taming Your Overconfidence

Developing self-confidence is a good thing. But in excess, it can be detrimental to your personal growth and even kill your self-esteem and, consequently, your self-worth. Overconfidence occurs when you are excessively confident or overly optimistic about yourself. This may be hazardous to your self-worth and overall well-being.

An overly confident man will cause more trouble than he solves problems. Overconfidence will kill your creativity and will lead you into a downward spiral. If you are overconfident, you may ignore advice from your peers, family, and colleagues, because you believe you can handle everything yourself, and you are convinced that your ability is enough to handle the situation at hand.

Taming your confidence is essential; you should maintain confidence levels that are within acceptable thresholds. The need to be better than the rest and to be recognized for what you do at the expense of others is a clear sign of overconfidence. There is a thin line separating overconfidence and arrogance. Overconfidence is the enemy of what you want and what you have. Overconfidence can cause you to lose everything you have worked tirelessly for over the years.

Overconfidence is the voice within that tells you that you are better than you are; it inhibits real success and prevents a direct and honest connection to the society around you. It is a conscious separation from everything. It prevents us from working collaboratively with other people.

You should suppress overconfidence early enough before the bad habits that come with it become innate. Overconfidence will forever impede your aspirations. Taming your overconfidence is a journey that will take longer, depending on how damaged your self-worth is. Many men are struggling unnecessarily, simply because they don't realize that overconfidence is causing the problems they are facing in life. You should be able to recognize overconfidence or ego and how to get it under control.

You can manage your confidence levels. But how do you know for sure if it has reached a level that you have to tame? Here are some signs that you need to work on your overconfidence:

• You are never satisfied with your accomplishments—you find yourself working toward a goal, telling yourself that once you reach it, you will be a happy man, and live a fulfilled life. But once you do, you remain unhappy. This is a sign of overconfidence and a damaged ego.

• You are always insecure and envious of others—this is depicted when you have the constant need to compare yourself to others to find satisfaction. You are never okay with where you are unless you are convinced that it is better than where someone else is. You derive happiness from knowing that you are smarter or better than others.

• You burn bridges on your way—this can be a long list of bad breakups, friendships falling apart after an argument, et cetera. These are signs that your confidence level is out of control. If you have trouble keeping healthy relationships, it means you are confident that you can work things out alone, and this is a limiting belief.

• You exhibit a lot of addiction to social media—overconfidence thrives on the instant gratification of social media. If you find yourself always reaching for something like your smartphone, it's a likely sign that your confidence level needs some work.

If these points apply to you, you will be required to tame your overconfidence. The good news is that it is possible to tame your overconfidence. All it needs is commitment. If you are willing to improve your life, self-worth, relationships, and your self-confidence, this book is perfect for you. It will give you practical advice to taming your overconfidence.

Overconfidence causes you to be arrogant. Confidence that we have discussed in the previous chapters is different from the arrogance that is depicted by overconfidence. You can be excessively confident about your skills or abilities. You may accept yourself completely without becoming arrogant in your interactions with others.

Some people will argue that overconfidence is not a bad thing. The same people would say that overconfidence is necessary to succeed. The idea of succeeding, in this example, would mean winning status, honor, and attaining material possessions or prestige. It is only when your confidence is enormous that you will be able to succeed on particular job paths or get to the top of the chain. For instance, in jobs where harming others is mandatory, reaching the top would mean sacrificing your respect of others for the sake of serving your overconfidence.

Ten Habits Necessary for Taming Overconfidence

Since your confidence levels are complicated and are multi-leveled, it is not practical to get rid of it all at once. It is not even humanly possible to achieve that. Below are habits that you can practice to tame your overconfidence:

1. Have Realistic Expectations for Your Confidence and Personal Goals

This will not happen instantly, and if you have unrealistic expectations you will only cause yourself unnecessary heartache. Instead, commit to improving yourself gradually, every day in small chunks—provided you are moving forward every day.

You can view the process of getting rid of limiting beliefs and destructive mental habits in the same way as removing a burdensome tree from the garden. Begin by identifying thoughts that exist to strengthen your overconfidence, and then detach from them, eventually getting to a place where you can let them go, seeing yourself as separate from the fake identity that your overconfidence brought about.

2. Practice Meditation

This is the leading method for noticing your overconfidence and separating yourself from it. Meditation is a great way to detach from habits that promote overconfidence. A number of religions sing the praises of meditation frequently, and for a good reason, since it pays off immensely to those who commit to it—you don't need to be religious to benefit.

3. Noticing Your Thoughts

Meditation, contrary to popular belief and rumor, isn't about trying to stop thinking. It's about learning to see your ideas. Once you begin to do this, you will see that most of these thoughts that cross your mind throughout the day seem to come out of nowhere, and many of them don't even make sense.

4. Eliminating the Constant Stream of Nonsense

You don't choose your thoughts, which is why advertising is a successful business. You are subjected to hundreds of things each day, often against your will, and this is even more apparent in the era of social media. How many times per day do you find yourself thinking of some random nonsense that you saw earlier and don't care about at all? The good news is that you don't have to be subjected to this, mindfulness will help you to tune out the excess "noise" from these sources.

5. Blocking Unworthy Thoughts

The idea here is not to stop the thoughts completely but to address them when they show up. With meditation, you can realize these thoughts when they manifest and accept then move past the ones that aren't worth your time.

6. Harnessing Empowering Thoughts

An average person is tossed around all day long by this cascade of thoughts, and meditation gives you back the power to be the one in control. You will start to recognize when your ego starts to try to take over, and you will be giving yourself the option of saying no.

7. Find a Creative Pursuit

Creativity is an excellent source of inspiration that can disengage you from the constant chatter of your confidence levels. People often believe that they are "not creative," but this isn't true. Every person is creative, and the only thing holding you back from thinking this is your overconfident tendencies.

8. Taking a Walk in Nature

Humans in modern times live in an unnatural environment and rarely see the outdoors. This leads to a lot of discomfort that you often don't even realize. To neutralize the overconfidence levels and become a healthier, more grounded individual, you must regain contact with your roots as a member of this planet and start going outside more.

9. Spend Some Time with Children

Children have less developed confidence levels, so they are truer and more themselves, something many adults have forgotten. Hanging out with them can really help you to begin thinking in a clearer and simpler way about what is really important in life.

10. Decluttering

Owning a lot of stuff is not a bad thing, but it can weigh on you, and pull you down, and intensify your overconfidence. It's too easy to start equating your own sense of worth with what you own when you have a lot of stuff. You become afraid of what would happen if you didn't have these things. In other words, you fear that the false confidence that you've built up would cease to exist if you didn't have the material possessions. When you offload some of the possessions, you will become less worried about material things, and at the same time, you will enjoy giving others the things you no longer need.

SECTION 3: Self-Discipline

Self-Discipline and Its Core Values

Self-discipline is the control you exert over yourself. For example, the power you have over your emotions, feelings, behaviors, activities, and even what you think. It entails avoiding unhealthy excesses that may result in negative consequences. If you are a self-disciplined man, you will easily control your urges to indulge in harmful or unconstructive activities that may negatively affect your productivity. You tend to stick to your mission and objectives.

From this definition, you may confuse self-discipline with willpower. Willpower is the ability to set a course of action and be sure that you will start it and manage it to the end. You can control any damaging or needless impulses, and have the ability to overcome procrastination and laziness, as well as the ability to arrive at a decision then follow through with perseverance to its logical end.

Self-discipline differs from this in the sense that willpower will get you started in setting your goals and remaining on course. But self-discipline is required if you wish to realize your true potential in life. Once willpower has placed you on the road, you need something to keep you going, and that is self-discipline. It gives you the stamina to persevere in whatever you do. It gives you the strength to withstand hardships, be they emotional or mental. Also, self-discipline gives you the ability to reject instant gratification for the greater good in the long run. This may require a lot of effort and time. Therefore, you will realize that there is a very thin line between self-discipline and willpower.

To develop a strong sense of discipline and willpower, you will become conscious of your internal subconscious impulses and gain the ability to discard them anytime they are not for your benefit. In essence, self-discipline coupled with strong willpower allows you to choose your behavior and reactions, instead of being enslaved by them. You feel more powerful and in charge of yourself and your surroundings when you muster self-discipline.

Self-discipline is critically essential if you want to get things done promptly, mainly because it helps you stay on the path to achieving your goals. So how can you build your self-discipline? Well, before we start discussing various ways and methods you can use to develop this ability, it is essential first to explain the reasons why most of us lack this key ability. Delving into these two aspects will help you understand the importance of developing self-confidence.

Six Reasons Why You Need Self-Discipline

The core value of self-discipline is success. Therefore, it is important to exercise discipline at every opportunity. Reasons for harnessing self-discipline in your life include:

1. Lack of it will mean you lack self-control. Thus, when working on something, you quickly get distracted and give in to your desires, urges, and feelings. You do not stay dedicated to your missions, and you quickly lose sight of what is essential and beneficial to you. Self-discipline seeks to reverse that; it helps you to stick to whatever it is you have planned to do, no matter the level of discomfort or difficulties that you face along the way.

When self-discipline is lacking, your chances of becoming sidetracked are high, meaning that you can forget long-term desires and goals forever. On the contrary, if you practice self-discipline, you will always achieve everything you desire in life.

2. Self-discipline will enable you to exercise control over yourself and avoid thinking or feeling negative. When you are self-disciplined, you think before acting, brainstorm quickly, think lucidly, focus on essential tasks, efficiently complete all the chores you have started, and successfully carry out your plans and decisions despite obstacles, hardships, and inconveniences that come your way.

3. Additionally, self-discipline helps you to make the right choices by evaluating things, by weighing their pros and cons; when you are self-disciplined, you seldom make erratic impulsive decisions.

4. Furthermore, self-discipline helps you to become happier and more peaceful. A study titled: *Yes, But Are They Happy? Effects of Trait Self-Control on Affective Well-Being and Life Satisfaction,* was conducted in 2013 by Wilhelm Hoffman, and showed that those who had high self-control were happier as compared to those who lacked self-control. According to the study, self-disciplined people deal with their goal conflicts a lot better, waste less time in unhealthy behaviors, and can make positive decisions easily. This, in turn, enhances their levels of inner peace and happiness.

5. Self-discipline can help you to avoid making decisions in a rash or an impulsive manner, making you fulfill promises that you set for yourself and others, and continue working on a project even when your enthusiasm has faded away. It is the one thing that will make you wake up every single morning to do some of the things that you feel you shouldn't be doing because of your lack of enthusiasm.

6. With self-discipline, you can build healthy relationships, command respect from others, and you can also manage your thoughts, reactions, and eventually achieve everything you have set your eyes and mind to.

From the above, it is clear that nurturing habits that enhance your self-discipline is the right step toward transforming your life.

Why Men Lack Self-Discipline

Even though self-discipline is a vital element that should be part of your personality, many men lack it and are extremely far from acquiring it. Ask yourself what makes it so impossible for you to overcome laziness, stop excessive eating, or stop smoking?

The answer is you don't have the self-discipline to do what should be done to realize your goals and desires. You need to know what is lacking to correctly address the situation. Here are the reasons why self-discipline may be lacking:

- **Self-Discipline Is Not a Built-In Ability**

Self-discipline is not something you are born with; it is something you work on and develop. Those who are disciplined have worked hard to build this strength and those who do not have it need to put in the effort to acquire it.

- **Negative Mental and Emotional Programming**

Not all of us have positive and healthy "mental programming." In childhood and throughout their lives, many people go through various terrible incidents that induce negative thinking, which shapes negative behaviors and keeps them from gaining self-discipline.

- **Negative Environments**

A positive environment is mandatory in the development of self-discipline and willpower. If the people around you are not supportive and constantly demoralize you, you will never be able to discern right and wrong and discipline yourself. If you are not lucky enough to reside in a positive environment, you need to work on creating one for yourself to gain self-discipline.

- **Fear of Failure**

The fear of failing at something prevents you from taking the initiative. When you cannot initiate tasks and activities, you cannot move toward your goals. This lowers your inner strength, an integral and essential part of developing willpower.

- **Laziness**

If you are incredibly lazy, you never feel like doing anything and are always procrastinating. Where there is procrastination, there cannot be self-discipline. To develop self-discipline, laziness and procrastination have to go: it is that simple.

- **Low Self-Esteem and Self-Confidence**

When you are not sure of yourself and do not highly value yourself, you cannot be confident of your abilities. When you are not aware of your strengths and lack confidence, developing the discipline to get things done will be a challenge. It is harder to develop the skills you need, because if you have low self-esteem and confidence, it will seem much easier to procrastinate even if the task is critical to your attainment of certain goals.

- **Easily Falling Prey to Temptation**

If you easily fall prey to different things that lure you away from your goal, your self-discipline is lacking. To gain restraint and self-will, it is essential to overcome your weaknesses and temptations.

- **A Lack of Purpose**

To be self-disciplined, your life must have a purpose, a goal you look forward to, and that you can stay dedicated to. On the contrary, if you do not know your lifelong objectives, and have not realized them yet, you are likely to be lacking self-discipline.

From the above, you have now noticed one or two reasons why your self-discipline is wanting. Lack of self-discipline reduces your chances of achieving whatever it is you wish to achieve in life. Therefore, self-discipline is a quality that you must adopt in your life.

Mindset Matters: Changing Your Limiting Beliefs

This section will show you the power of your beliefs. You may be aware of these beliefs or not, but either way, limiting beliefs affect what your goals are in life. Changing your self-limiting views, even in the simplest way possible, can have positive effects on your self-confidence.

Your personality emanates from your mindset. Everything that is preventing you from fulfilling your set objectives is based on your beliefs and mindset.

Muhammad Yunus once said: "My greatest challenge has been to change the mindset of people." He goes on to say that, "Mindsets play strange tricks on us. We see things the way our minds have instructed our eyes to see."

Everyone has a biased view of the world. This is because your childhood experiences have shaped your beliefs in life, how you see things, and how you perceive reality. For example, if you lived in poverty all your life, with sexual and emotional abuse, you will never believe in the goodness that life can bring until you choose to do so.

This means that your thoughts are a significant factor that affect your mindset and how you view life. For example, you may not have grown up in a hardship neighborhood, but you saw a friend or neighbor who was once prosperous, suddenly becoming poor in a snap. This will make you think and believe that it is possible to rise and fall quickly. When you think a lot about it, you will fear that it may happen to you. And gradually, you will start believing in it, and your mind will start looking for ways to make the belief come to pass.

You may not be able to control a lot that happens in your life, but one thing you can control is your thoughts. Your subconscious mind can't quickly tell the difference between what is real and what is an illusion created by your imagination. The mind will accept the input you give it and will act accordingly to process those inputs.

Here, the decision is yours. This section will help you to decide whether you will continue to hold on to the wrong mindset about yourself—by continuing to let the world or your past shape your confidence—or you will act to improve it. If you wish to change your mindset, below are some of the negative beliefs that you need to get rid of before installing new views:

Three Bad Mindsets That You Should Avoid

- Perfection

This is one of the wrong mindsets to have, as it can reduce your self-confidence. A misconception is that you are good only when you are "perfect." Of course, you will not be confident when you mess up something, but it doesn't mean that you can't develop self-confidence. Perfectionism can compromise your self-esteem. If you peg your confidence on "being perfect," it means you will never be confident in your entire life, because no one is perfect.

- That a Mindset is Permanent

You may believe that your fate is cast in stone and that you cannot change anything about yourself. You tend to have the mindset that this is just: "How God made you." Such a statement shows that your situation is permanent and that it cannot be changed. This limiting belief will make you feel like a lesser being. With such low self-esteem, it will prevent you from becoming confident about yourself. If you have such a fixed mindset, you will often think that striving to be self-confident is a waste of time. Affected men will avoid anything that requires extreme effort to change for the better.

- **Achievement Equals Confidence**

Your achievements can, indeed, make you confident. But this should not be confused to mean that you have first to achieve in order to be confident. On the contrary, you may realize so much success in life, only because you were confident in the first place. If you achieve without confidence, that is considered an accidental achievement. Take an example of the late Kobe Bryant, who developed confidence in playing basketball from childhood. When he joined the NBA, he was confident enough to achieve the best results, since he had developed the art from his childhood days. You will need to be confident in yourself before you can achieve your set objectives.

Seven Ways to Develop Confidence with the Right Mindset

There are several ways of avoiding a bad mindset. Some are cheap and easy to implement, but some can be very hard and costly. Here are some practical ways of uprooting a bad mindset that is preventing you from becoming confident and being an "Alpha" man:

1. Practice Positive Affirmations

Jimmy Connors once said: "Use it or lose it." As far as your thoughts and mindsets are concerned, the less you exercise your mind, the weaker it becomes. And as the mind becomes weak, it will be prone to be affected by external factors, which will significantly affect your confidence. By using positive affirmations (positive self-talk), you will exercise your mind toward being confident about yourself. It is an effective way of influencing your subconscious mind to be more confident. Positive affirmations are best used with a partner. Since you are not perfect, by including a trusted friend or member of the family, you will benefit from their help as they will remind you when you go astray from your goals. A partner will tell you to uproot the negative mindset if they see it coming back.

2. Stop Thinking About Negative Mindsets

Always loop the bad mindset ideas from your mind. Avoid engaging your mind to think about the wrong mindsets. If you think of why you can't be confident, you will forever question your self-worth. This is like meditating or thinking of a particular thing, so repeatedly that it becomes a part of you. The less you think of the limiting beliefs, the more you develop your self-worth. If done over time, you will be able to increase your self-esteem.

3. Interrogating Yourself

The best way of avoiding a negative mindset is to challenge it. You can achieve this by continually questioning yourself about the benefits you are deriving from the limiting mindset. This should be done regularly, so that eventually, you will find yourself completely eliminating the limiting mindsets that affect your confidence.

4. Keep the Right Company

To develop your confidence, you should try hanging out with confident men. Transference of spirit will happen when you hang around highly confident people. You will be able to copy what they are doing, and in a short while, and with practice, it will become part of you. The good thing is that with confidence, once you master it, it is impossible to lose it. But again, even on the acquisition, you must practice very often. Experience, they say, is an excellent teacher. But still, you can learn a lot from other people's experiences. This way, you will be able to avoid trying silly things that have already been experienced by your friends, and the repercussions shared with you.

5. Seek Excellence

The journey to self-worth requires that you strive to excel in life, rather than being perfect. As we discussed earlier, seeking perfection is the highest confidence killer. On the other hand, excellence is concerned with you giving your best in the tasks that you handle, whether it's work or family, sports, or even schoolwork. Excelling in what you do is a significant boost to your confidence. The secret of excellence is making the most of what you have in your hands. Excellence entails all the choices you make.

6. Practice Continuous Improvement

Excelling is the first step in building your self-worth. But after that, you need to continuously excel and improve from your scores from the last count. It is common to find that a costly phone that you purchased recently might be considered old and useless in less than three months. Now back to you, the skills that you have achieved will be outdated in a few months, and this will significantly affect your ability to handle tasks excellently, and consequently, it will affect your self-worth.

For example, social media has recently become a force that shapes personal lives and businesses. The need for social media experts has increased significantly. Many are catching up on this demand and have learned how to be proficient marketers. Therefore, if you are in the marketing profession, you ought to understand the trends in social media marketing and how you can effectively tap into them to increase your business worth. Being on top of the game is a confidence booster. If you don't continuously invest in your personal or professional growth, you run the risk of losing your confidence in the long term.

Conversely, personal growth plays a significant role in boosting your self-confidence. You are way ahead of many by just reading this book. Reading is the most critical and straightforward means of personal growth. By reading books, you can access the minds of many; it also provides you with the luxury of convenience since you can read a book at your own time and pace.

7. Visualize

Another way to have a positive mindset is to program your mind through visualization. This is the ability to create a precise and vivid mental image of what you want in life. Create a clear mental picture of yourself performing at your optimum level in any given situation, and visualize it turning out precisely the way you want it to. That way, your confidence levels will increase, since in these visualizations you will consider yourself worthy and contributing to the world positively.

Therefore, we have seen that maintaining a positive mindset and avoiding limiting beliefs is the key to developing self-worth or self-confidence. Positivity is the act of looking at life or the things that happen in your life from a positive perspective.

Maintaining a positive mindset does not mean that you are blind to the negativity that exists in the world. It just means dwelling on the possible or actual good things that can emanate from events, actions, situations, or people. In this section, you have learned how limiting beliefs set the course for your life. What you believe permeates every part of your adult life.

Mindset Self-Test

To establish whether you are in the right state of mind to handle what life throws at you, you need to assess yourself by asking yourself these questions:

✔ Do you have peace of mind?

✔ Are you in control of your own life?

✔ Do you plan your life well?

✔ Do you know how to achieve your full potential?

✔ Do you like yourself?

✔ Are you concerned about what people may think of you?

✔ Are you willing to let bygones be bygones and make changes in your life?

✔ Do you expect the best of yourself?

✔ Do you regularly practice positive thinking and positive affirmations?

✔ Are you destined for success?

✔ Are you continuously improving and growing toward your potential?

The questions above will help you to program your mind and even let you know what to think. You are a result of everything you have believed in until now. What you will grow into in the future will ultimately be the result of the content in your mind.

The law of belief states that whatever you believe with feeling becomes your reality, and if you wish to change your reality, you must change your beliefs about yourself first. Additionally, the law of expectation states that whatever you expect with confidence becomes your self-fulfilling prophecy, and for this reason, you must assume the best from others and every situation. Lastly, the law of attraction states that you inevitably attract into your life the people and circumstances that harmonize with your dominating thoughts. To attract different people or situations, you have to change the way you think.

Thus, nobody remains the same for an extended period. You are continually changing in the direction of your dominant thoughts and objectives. You should keep in mind the kind of person you would like to be and the goals you want to accomplish. To develop self-worth, you have to let go of the past. You have to develop new habits and patterns of thinking about yourself. This is done by thinking, talking, and acting in a manner that is consistent with the person you wish to be in the future, with the attributes and characteristics that you would like to adopt.

Mental Toughness: The Zero F*cks Method

Mental toughness is your ability to deal with pressures, stressors, and challenges and to get the best possible results, despite the circumstances that you might find yourself in. It is also defined as the ability to rise after failures and setbacks, and the resolve to spot and take hold of the opportunities that come up.

Also, mental toughness can be defined as a "character in action." This definition was coined by the famous football coach, Vince Lombardi. Mental toughness is essential because it compensates for the lack of skill, natural ability, and strength. You have often heard it said that the people at the top in any field whatsoever are not the most talented; they are those who stayed and kept at it despite the challenges they faced. Mental toughness prevents you from becoming a quitter. In the documentary *Pumping Iron* (1977), Arnold Schwarzenegger says that you must go on and on, not caring what happens. This resolve is what gets an athlete through the competition in a marathon—you must keep running until you get to the end.

Therefore, whatever you call it—balls, guts, wits, or will—this is what we are calling "mental toughness." The question now is: how do you become mentally healthy and tough?

If you ask around, many coaches, athletes, and corporate leaders will tell you that mental toughness is inborn or developed in the earlier stages of life, depending on the environment a child grows up in. It is challenging to transform people, but with the realization that you are capable of improving the various aspect of your life, this should be followed with the utmost optimism.

Skills That Define a Mentally Tough Man

Mentally tough people quickly rise to positions of influence and power in business, leadership, sports, and even in life. Observing them keenly, experts have outlined some skills common in all of them.

These defining skills include but are not limited to:

• **A hyper-focus.** This is the ability to perform at peak levels with ease without giving in to distractions and with a clarity of mind. This is called "being within the zone."

• **A winning mindset.** A winning mindset is an attitude that you must win or at least operate at the maximum possible efficiency level, maintaining consistency. To do this, you must have a strong belief and faith in your field of expertise and skills despite the challenges presented to you.

• **Willpower.** As pointed out earlier, willpower combines effort, intention, and courage. The aim is the "will" in willpower. It is the insistence on staying on the same task until all the work is done. The effort you put into doing something is the power. It propels you into achieving what is required of you despite the challenges you encounter. Courage is the readiness to bear up all the fear and other emotions that you need to accomplish the task.

• **Composed.** A mentally tough person has to keep calm under pressure. As the situation heightens and everyone else is freaking out, the individual remains calm, takes time to assess the situation, and then makes the best possible move. You must stay engaged in the case no matter how high the pressure rises.

• **Lose well.** Along with the mindset of a winner is the ability to accept that the performer is capable of failure. Sometimes, even with the highest focus and costly investment of skills and resources, you can fail to meet the set objective. However, the trick lies in your ability to extract lessons and values from each experience and to channel them into the next trial, for continued success.

- **Own up.** To develop mental toughness, you need to own up to every situation, both the good and the bad. A mentally healthy person is ready and willing to take up that responsibility and pressure. You believe that whatever the challenges and the odds, you must come up with a solution. In case of failure, you will take stock, evaluate your steps to see where you went wrong, gather lessons from it, and then move on past it. You know how to overcome negative emotions and thoughts effectively.
- **Preparation.** Preparedness involves lots of planning. A good man will plan early enough. You will also create a backup plan that can be activated if, indeed, the original plan fails or it just will not work. Planning and preparation of this nature allow you to remain at ease, regardless of the situation. In addition, the task itself can be fully recovered and completed, without having to return to the starting point. What's more, your spirit is not crushed, and the performance rhythm is not affected much by the perceived loss and failure.
- **Ready to take on the challenge.** A mentally tough person does not whimper. You do not whine. Whatever comes your way, you readily welcome it. Be it having to stay up late to work on some project, be it having to take on more people for training, be it running several extra miles. Whatever it is, you have a "bring it on" attitude, and this produces exposure, experience, and success.
- **Stress optimization.** This is the ability to manage pressure and stress during any event, without any anxiety, fear, or doubt—or at least maintaining your performance undeterred by them. An individual who has learned how to optimize stress will take advantage of a stressful environment and come up with results that others could not have presented under similar conditions.

- **Stretch out the limits.** This is your ability to exact maximum physical effort even in the face of mental and physical stress. You could be in pain or physical discomfort and commit yourself to give the best performance irrespective of the situation at hand. We have seen athletes in severe physical pain go on to finish the race on the tracks.

We have seen above the skills that you need to develop, to claim that you are a mentally tough man. Now, we look at the methods used to achieve mental toughness. Below are the "no f*ck" approaches or habits that you should practice daily to become a mentally tough person:

Routine Habits of Mentally Tough Men

If you are a mentally tough man, there is a high chance that you were not born tough. You have developed these critical habits and have been practicing them every day, thus setting you apart from other men. These habits are discernible in the way you approach life and the challenges that come to you. A mentally tough man's methods are usually different from the approach of an average man.

As Henry Ford of Ford Motors once put it: "Failure is simply the opportunity to begin again, this time more intelligently." Once you have identified the mistakes that prevent you from succeeding, you will need to develop the right mental attitude to help you navigate through failure and to overcome challenges and differing opinions, and the bad habits that stifle you.

Here are some no f*ck habits that you need to practice daily to develop the mental strength and toughness that you require:

- **Practice gratitude.** As a mentally healthy person, you will count your blessings every day, rather than your problems, to help keep your life in perspective. The "attitude of gratitude" brings the joy that eliminates all negative feelings, and elevates your moods, in readiness for the tasks at hand.

- **Take on challenges.** To a mentally tough person, a challenge is only an opportunity to become stronger. With each victory, you become more confident and better at what you are doing.
- **Maintain healthy boundaries.** Emotional, social, and physical boundaries create the room a tough-minded person needs to grow. Even though saying "no" might disappoint you if you are trying to get past the limits, you are happy to take that risk, for the sake of securing success in the future.
- **Maintain personal power.** A strong person does not allow a negative person to exert any control or influence. You are also not willing to use other people as excuses for why you are being held back or dragged down; you take full responsibility for your actions.
- **Only concentrate on things you have power over.** Mentally tough people know the value of being continually effective and productive in their roles. This can be achieved only when you focus on the things you can control, rather than wasting precious time thinking about current or future storms that you have no control over. You will expend energy in preparing for and responding to something that happens, rather than in trying to prevent it from happening.

For instance, if the country expects to go into a recession, you don't go about trying to prevent it; it would be a complete waste of time. Instead, you work on managing your organization and planning on the response the company will give when the recession is here. Will production decrease? How will that affect the market? A stable mind will think about those issues.

- **Make peace with the past.** The past is only essential to a tough-minded person for its lessons. You reflect on it so you can learn from it, not regret your actions or those of others. You do not hold grudges either.
- **Learn from mistakes.** Instead of beating yourself up because of an error, a mentally healthy person will focus on the lessons learned.

You will take full responsibility for your behavior and choose to move forward, positively.

- **Take calculated risks.** Each decision a mentally tough person makes must be backed by logic so that each risk taken is calculated for its possible pay off and losses. As such, you are willing to step out of your comfort zone to look for non-traditional opportunities and solutions that will propel you to success.
- **Have alone time.** Any successful person will tell you of the value of alone time. When you are left alone to your thoughts, you can meditate, journal, plan, and reflect. Some time of solitude is essential for any growing and innovative mind.
- **Take full responsibility.** As mentioned in a previous point, as a mentally tough person, you will take charge of your life. You do not wait for opportunities to be handed to you, nor do you sit around whining about what should have been or what is owed to you. You go out and make it happen.
- **Persevere.** Strong people are believers of the fact that good things take time, and that they are worth waiting for. You will be persistent and patient as you strive to achieve particular milestones in your life journey.
- **Be realistic in your optimism.** Mentally tough people are not daydreamers. You refuse to be put down by pessimistic opinions and predictions, but still, will not allow yourself to be overconfident.
- **Allow discomfort.** Pain is a necessary part of the process, and a mentally tough person is not afraid to experience some. It may mean getting overly tired or resisting the urge to be gratified instantly. This requires a great deal of self-discipline to endure the discomfort.
- **Work on unhealthy habits.** As a mentally tough person, you will not allow your unhealthy habits to get in the way of your success. You understand that the mind has the capacity to become the worst enemy to your success. Therefore, you are continually working against overindulging in food, your hot temper, hitting the snooze

button, watching mind-altering films, and other negative behaviors that limit success.

- **Use your mental capacity wisely.** As a mentally tough person, you will not complain about things that you cannot change, or keep rehashing something that happened in the past. You know better than to devote your energy to activities and tasks that are unproductive. Your limited resources, like time and energy, are used sparingly and in the right manner.

Five Self-Discipline Habits for Daily Improvement

In the previous section, we have explored why self-discipline may be lacking. It is a quality that must be acquired first of all by assessing yourself and then practicing the habits that will improve your self-discipline. Since self-discipline is an excellent quality, you should not wait for it to come naturally, because it won't. Drop all your excuses and practice self-discipline habits daily.

Start by identifying your objectives and goals, as well as determining why you wish to get rid of all the wrong behaviors. Avoiding excuses is among the many habits that you should practice daily to become a disciplined man.

Below is a detailed description of the five self-discipline habits that you should practice daily:

1. Take action. Don't wait for the right time—it is common to come across advice that tells you to do something when it feels right and stop when you don't feel like doing it. It is said that you should follow your gut. Unfortunately, this is based on emotions, which are often unstable and highly unpredictable. Every man has a rollercoaster of emotions. Developing self-discipline is about learning how to get past the blockade that you create, like waiting for the right time to do something.

As described earlier, self-discipline is what keeps you focused on your goals even when you no longer feel enthusiastic. This means that emotions shouldn't be a determining factor on whether you will get started at something or not. As such, you are waiting for the right feeling or time, and this is a wrong approach to develop all the self-discipline that you need in life.

Choosing to work or not to work on a task based on the comfort it offers is the wrong approach to doing anything, and it is a tactic that can prevent you from gaining self-discipline.

If you are of the mindset that you should wait for the right time and emotion to do something, counter that by revisiting your "Why?". Of course, when you were developing your list of reasons for pursuing a goal, you never factored your emotions into that, so why should they be a determinant factor when it comes to getting things done? But how can you overcome the habit of waiting for the right feeling and time? By taking action, even if it is uncomfortable to do so.

2. Drop your habit of making excuses. Next, you need to discard your unhealthy behavior of making excuses for delaying a task. This has everything to do with procrastination. You cannot go far in your quest to build your self-discipline if you continuously procrastinate. The reason you've been struggling over the years to achieve your goals is probably that you make excuses for not starting (which amounts to procrastination).

Let me give you an example of the form that excuses take. "I won't be able to go for a jog because my jogging partner will not come," or "I won't go to the gym for 30 minutes today because I want to go for one-hour next time." Well, all these are excuses. However, if you want to transform yourself into a version that gives no excuses, you will need to be very honest with yourself to determine the real reason why you don't want to do something that needs to be done to achieve your goal.

For instance, if you come up with an excuse like, "I won't go out for a run now since it is freezing outside," then you should be honest with yourself and state the real reason for not jogging. Tell yourself,

"I am not going jogging because I am feeling lazy and lack the will to do something healthy."

Nobody will admit to being lazy. That's why this realization will push you out of your self-defined comfort zone of laziness—to prove to yourself that you are not lazy. With time, it will be easy to transform your life when you stop giving excuses for your inability to take action.

3. Develop an action plan and take action. This is a habit that you need to develop and practice daily. To develop self-discipline, you will have to work on your personal goals by preparing an action plan for them. Here is how to go about it:

✔ Make your action plan. You can create a tabular action plan or use Excel or MS Word to make one. Find out what steps you need to carry out and in what order they must be performed to do what needs to be done to achieve a particular goal.

Make sure to add essential columns or sections, such as "action to be taken," "time to start the task," "potential problems I could face," "strategies I can adopt for overcoming issues," and "progress report." Next, you need to fill the columns with appropriate content.

✔ Prepare yourself to take action. Once you have filled in the information required to achieve a goal, next is to take action. But before you do that, ensure to go through the document to "absorb" everything that's in it. You should also use this review to identify any flaws in the document, and if you find any, ensure to make the necessary changes.

Next, you need to prepare yourself to take action. In this case, action refers to the steps to be taken to achieve your objectives. For instance, your efforts could include such activities as finding a good yoga class and enrolling in one to start your journey to losing weight with yoga—if that's what you want to achieve. And as you do this, you should let your action plan guide you to action. But if the action plan is not sufficiently detailed so that it has the specifics or even the smallest of details, you can get someone to help you come up with ideas for taking action.

✔ Anticipate problems that may occur and find solutions. You need to consider any potential issue(s) that you are likely to face when working on your action plan and devise strategies that will help you to overcome such issues.

For example, if you worry that you'll switch off the alarm when it rings at 5 am and drift off to sleep again, then a potential problem could be "I will probably fall asleep." Then identify any workable solution that could help you to tackle this issue. For instance, you could ask your partner or your roommate to wake you up and ensure that you don't go back to sleep. You could have an accountability partner who ensures you follow your action plan. They could call you at your exercising time and keep ringing until you actually wake up. Think of similar strategies like these to instill respect in your action plan.

✔ Regularly review your plan. You cannot know how well you are doing if you don't track your progress. This means that you won't be able to tell whether you are really following your action plan.

Therefore, it is important that you make the necessary plans to know how well you are performing with regard to following your action plan. For instance, if you wanted to lose weight (say 15 pounds in two months), you will need to determine how often you will weigh yourself to determine your progress. If you notice any flaws in your action plan, this is the best time to fix that. This will increase your chances of following the procedure and nurturing your self-discipline.

✔ Never repeat mistakes. You are bound to make mistakes along the way. That is okay. Never put yourself down, criticize, or hate yourself upon making a mere mistake. All you need to do is to get up, inspire yourself, and keep pushing. Research shows that when you make a mistake, you are likely to shut down or attempt to solve the problem. If you concentrate on your mistakes and struggle t0 correct them, you are most likely to succeed, as opposed to overlooking your flaws or ignoring them altogether.

✔ When you discover your mistake, take some time to reflect on the mistakes as objectively as possible and avoid blaming yourself or criticizing yourself for any wrongdoing. You want to encourage yourself into action, not put yourself down for your flaws. Reflect on the positives and the benefits that will come with nurturing self-discipline. This will give you a glimpse of the bigger picture, hence increasing your chances of feeling motivated to action, as opposed to feeling bad for making mistakes.

4. Practice overcoming temptations. As you work toward building self-discipline, you should anticipate facing many "temptations." Changing yourself from the person that you were in the beginning—a person who lacked self-discipline—to one who has excellent self-discipline, is going to take some time and will have a steep learning curve.

You shouldn't expect to move from one end to the other end of the spectrum instantly without facing any temptations to go back to the habits that you are so used to.

Here are a few strategies on how to overcome temptations and stay committed to your goal:

✔ Detach yourself from the attractions that lead to temptations.

✔ Envisage yourself resisting temptation.

✔ Weigh instant gratification against the long-term consequences.

✔ Keep yourself busy with important stuff to avoid falling into temptation.

5. Inspire and develop yourself. Self-discipline is not only created by eliminating temptations from your life; making the right decisions; following your action plans; and dumping excuses. There's something else you need to do as well: nurture yourself and keep yourself motivated.

Gaining self-discipline can be quite challenging, mainly if you are not used to it. You'll make mistakes in the beginning and probably even consider giving up. But since this mostly happens when you don't encourage yourself, you need to come up with creative strategies that you can follow to keep yourself motivated as you work toward transforming your self-discipline.

Here are some sure ways of getting yourself inspired:

✔ Compliment yourself every day.

✔ Take good care of yourself.

✔ Get enough sleep.

✔ Exercise regularly.

Power Goals: Thinking Long Term for Success

To be successful in life, you must create a clear vision of what you want in life. Set clear goals. From the previous chapters, you have learned about ways of eliminating limiting beliefs. Now you can firm up your personal goals and bring them to life in a way that will register in your unconscious mind and help it happen.

Having a clear image of your goals and objectives into the future will inspire you and keep you focused on doing everything necessary to achieve the goal. This last section of this book will guide you through:

- Why setting goals is key to long term success.
- What works well in setting goals?
- You will learn the five conditions necessary for successful goals.
- You will learn how to make your goals compelling.
- You will learn how to install your goals for long-term success.

Set Your Goals

You should set your goals the right way for success. There is a proper way, and there is a wrong way of setting your goals. The right approach should be the SMART way because it allows you to plan, act, and analyze the progress you have made.

You are more likely to succeed in life if you are good at analyzing your progress and keeping track of things that you are supposed to achieve to succeed.

The journey to success will always start with goal setting. These goals will become the central focus of your life. You should choose as few goals as possible, since the more goals you set, the more it will take you to accomplish each.

Because you need to limit your attention to a few goals as possible, you'll undoubtedly have to give up working on other, less important goals. If you fear doing so, you need to ask yourself if spreading yourself thin until now has helped you to achieve anything in life.

How to Set the Right Goal

The goal or goals you choose to focus on have to be so important that they can transform your life. They also need to provide more benefits than neglecting your less vital goals. In other words, as an example, you have to feel good forgoing or delaying becoming a great golf player and going to the gym to develop a six-pack in exchange for moving into your dream house.

Common Transformational Goals

1. Getting in shape. This includes: losing weight, exercising more, replacing bad habits with healthy ones. If your long-term well-being is in danger, no other goal is as important as following your doctor's orders. Forgo any other aspirations and make it your top priority.

2. Building a business, advancing your career, or rebranding yourself. This includes learning skills and acquiring the credentials that are needed to change your occupation.

3. Finding a significant other, starting a family, taking care of your children, and other goals related to relationships. Just like taking care of your health, this can sometimes be more crucial than any other purpose. Saving your marriage is more important than developing your career.

4. Learning a skill or developing a trait that will produce a profound change in your life or give you more opportunities. This could include: eliminating procrastination from your life, learning a foreign language, overcoming shyness, becoming a professional public speaker, or overcoming a paralyzing phobia.

5. **Lifestyle goals, like traveling, buying a house and moving to your dream location.** Ensure that you can't imagine your life without making this goal or goals come true. This is imperative; if you don't think of your goal as a necessity in your life and an absolute must, you won't achieve it.

When I set a goal to become a successful entrepreneur, it wasn't just a wish. There was no possible scenario in which I wouldn't eventually own a profitable business. I was unable to imagine myself working for somebody else.

If you don't have such a deep conviction and desire for the goal or goals you want to achieve, reconsider them. The entire strategy is based on the assumption that you'll either eventually make it happen or die trying (and "eventually" here means that you'll try over and over, even if it's going to take you decades).

You must set clear goals, since they give you direction. When you know what your goals are, you will see the path you have to follow to get there—and you have something to aim for, so you can make corrections if you get blown off your path. Having a sense of purpose is a fundamental human need. Without this, you become unhappy. With setting goals, you will be more flexible and resilient and will be able to cope with changing conditions as you continuously develop.

How to Select the Goals to Pursue

What happens when you have several goals to pursue, and you are not sure which goals should be dropped and which should wait? There are various techniques that you can use to decide. Below are some:

- **Try flipping a coin.** This technique sounds ridiculous, but it should be approached with an open mind. If you need to decide between two goals, assign goals to each side of the coin and flip it. You'll know which objective is closer to your heart before the coin even lands, because you'll find yourself rooting for it. Pay attention to that emotional response that occurs while you're waiting to see the outcome of the coin toss.

If you don't have a coin nearby, use an online randomizer, or take two pieces of paper, write down the goals and ask another person to choose one of them without showing them the answers. Again, pay attention to what you are hoping the result will be.

This approach often works better than analyzing each goal and trying to make a logical decision. It could be because when it comes to setting goals that matter most to you, your gut usually knows best.

- **Think about your most critical values.** Another technique that can help you narrow down your list of goals or prioritize them is to think about your key benefits.

For me, one of my top values is personal freedom; hence my goal was to become a successful entrepreneur.

What is it for you? Is the current state of things preventing you from fully embracing your most crucial values in your everyday life?

For example, if excitement is one of your top values, but you work in a soul-sucking corporation, it will clash with your values for the rest of your life until you do something about it. This indicates that finding a more exciting job might be a good goal to choose as your primary objective.

- **Goals that you can't wait to achieve.** It's generally easy to assess whether somebody cares about something if one looks at their patience for it. If you have a history of giving up after experiencing the first failure, the chances are good that the goal you've chosen is not your priority. On the other hand, if you refuse to give in (even when everybody around you doubts in your ability to succeed), it's an indicator that you're working on the right goal.

Now you know how to set the right goals and which goals to drop. The next step is how to prioritize the goals and how to make sure they're realistic for you. Here, the two crucial questions to ask yourself are "when" and "how" to start.

Before starting the journey to success, and working toward the set goals, you should ask yourself the following questions:

1. Will the prevailing negative circumstances pose a challenge? More often than not, you probably won't regret starting sooner rather than later. However, in some instances, waiting might be a more reasonable option.

2. Have you slept on the job? Many books will teach excitedly about how you should start it now, right away, with no thought on your part. I've found from my personal experience that it's helpful to sleep on any new goal you have chosen, before taking action.

First, the next morning you'll probably see it from a slightly different perspective, which might give you better ideas on how to proceed. There will be more logic involved in your thought processes and it won't be mostly from your emotional side. Second, if you're not even half as fired up as you were the day before, chances are it was only a spur-of-the-moment idea that doesn't lend itself to a long-term plan.

3. Are you okay with the dark side of working toward accomplishing this goal? This is the final question you should ask yourself before commencing to pursue your goals. When you're excited about setting a new purpose and changing your life, it's easy to fall victim to confirmation bias, in which you exclusively seek information that confirms your beliefs, while rejecting alternative or contrary knowledge.

Bonus – Top Ten Tips to Be a Confident Man

1. Believe That You CAN Make Good Decisions

The key to self-confidence and self-esteem is to believe that you *can* make those good decisions. Approaches based on mindfulness, focusing on the moment and positive affirmations that you can do it, all encourage a belief in yourself.

2. Tune the Negativity Out

In conjunction with the first tip, you must learn to tune negativity out. Be mindful of what has happened previously but keep an eye on the here and now—you can choose not to listen to ugliness and negativity from others, and from within yourself too.

3. Embrace and Learn from Mistakes

Everyone has made mistakes, but there is no shame in it. Push embarrassment to one side and embrace those mistakes; ask yourself what you learned from making them.

4. Focus on the Good

You must focus on your personal, physical, and intellectual assets when you review yourself. There must be positive things that you can say; nobody's life is all negative!

5. Practice Gratitude

This will positively and directly impact your self-esteem. What you are grateful for? What are the good things in your life? Do this while using mindfulness—you might be surprised at the answers.

6. Change Your Mental Self-Talk

Look in the mirror; look hard at yourself and then say something positive about your body, mind, personality, feelings, et cetera. If you can't, you need to switch off the "tape" of negative self-talk and turn on that positive one.

7. Change is Constant – Accept and Embrace It

We all change all of the time and what you see of yourself today will be different tomorrow, even if it is a minor change. Ask yourself what you are doing to bring about positive changes. Are you working hard on your body, mind, and spirit?

8. You ARE Worthy of Feeling Happiness – Accept It!

Happiness is an important part of life, but you won't attract success unless and until you believe that you are worthy of that happiness. There is a big difference between deserving happiness and being worthy of it—when you are worthy, you can absorb that happiness completely into your being.

9. Be Aware of Self-Care

Self-care is an important part of life. Whether it is through physical activity, body-building, diet, even personal grooming and taking care of your mental health. Invest the resources and the time into self-care and bring about positive changes and wellness.

10. Embrace Imperfections

Nobody is perfect, no matter how much they think they are. Every flaw you identify in yourself is likely one shared by other men—but ask yourself this—are the flaws really all that bad? Can you accept them as part of who you are? Your imperfections are a part of who you are. Embrace them!

Conclusion

Now that you have read the book, followed through the exercises provided, and identified what you need to increase your self-worth, it is time to go and practice!

Start adopting the simple strategies recommended here, and you will gradually see the benefits. As you watch these benefits accrue, you will develop a positive attitude toward change, and thus your self-esteem will improve.

Although it is important to note that these changes do not happen overnight, you should be patient enough and understand that it takes time to be the person you desire to be—but the results are so worthwhile.

As your self-esteem and self-confidence increase, you will experience increased growth that will lead to greater happiness in life. Getting started in the journey to self-worth is the hardest part; therefore, I suggest that you apply the tips presented in this book immediately. The tips are proven, and they work, but remember— they may not work for everyone. The suggestions offered in this book should also not be applied all at once. Create a plan that will help you to logically and sequentially implement the tips gradually.

The most important part is to make an effort to transform yourself, and you will feel the transformation taking place sooner than you envisaged. Try spending a few days working on one or two tips. Once you are in sync with the process, then try another one until they all become second nature. Your confidence will increase, and you will feel good about yourself and your life.

Additionally, keep a confidence journal. Just practice writing down ten things that you feel confident about. If done daily, it will change the way you think and feel about everything. I recommend you write your journal just before you go to bed. This way, the things you have written will flow into your subconscious mind as you sleep. You will not only wake up more confident, but you will also be happier with your achievements of the previous day, and you will have motivation and a clear plan for the next day.

In a nutshell:

✔ You hold the power to transform how you feel.

✔ Never feel bad for putting your needs first.

✔ You will not be selfish if you consider your needs first.

✔ Always try to be gentle on yourself; there is only one version of you in this world. So, take good care of it.

✔ Never hate the skin you are in.

Self-confidence is not engraved in men; thus, it can be enhanced or lost at any time. It is mostly affected by external factors that will make you believe that you don't have control over them.

Finally, confidence is within every man, but sometimes when the world is throwing you all manner of challenges, it can fade. Apply the tips discussed in this book when you are feeling less confident. It is not hard to acquire confidence, but if you don't have enough of it, succeeding in life can be difficult. You need the desire or drive to achieve confidence as a man and the persistence to stay at it until you get it. Your ideas, reflection, and thoughts can build your self-confidence, but you have to be aware of these to reach their full benefit.

By reading *Self-Confidence for Men: Unleash the Lion within and See How Your Mental Toughness, Self-Esteem, Mindset, Self-Discipline, and Dating Life Transforms,* you've already taken the first step on your journey. We hope you take full advantage of this book's structure, as you embrace your inner strength and develop your self-worth. Good luck!

Sources

1. Burton, K., & Platts, B. (2012). *Confidence for Dummies.* Wiley.
2. Schuster, S. (2018). *22 Habits of People With Low Self-Esteem.* The Mighty. Retrieved 11 February 2020, from https://themighty.com/2018/10/low-self-esteem-habits/.
3. Goldsmith, B. (2010). *100 Ways to Boost Your Self-confidence: Believe in Yourself and Others Will Too.* Career Press.
4. McGee, P. (2012). *Self-confidence: The Remarkable Truth of Why a Small Change Can Make a Big Difference.* Capstone.
5. Smith, E. (2018). *How Self-doubt Manifests in Men Versus Women.* Devex. Retrieved 12 February 2020, from https://www.devex.com/news/how-self-doubt-manifests-in-men-versus-women-92506.
6. Pollack, B. (2019). *Male Body Image and Body Dissatisfaction.* Mirror Mirror Eating Disorder Help. Retrieved 13 February 2020, from https://www.mirror-mirror.org/body-image-men.htm.
7. Blumer, C. (1934). *Discipline and Self-Discipline. The Australian Quarterly, Vol. 6 (Issue 23)*, 116. Australian Institute of Policy and Science. Retrieved 13 February 2020, from, https://doi.org/10.2307/20629153.
8. Bale, C. (2016). *From Shy Guy To Ladies Man – Memoirs Of A Male Seducer.* Ronlif Publishers.

Part 2: Self-Esteem for Men

An Essential Self-Help Guide to Building Alpha Male Habits that will Improve Your Mental Toughness, Confidence, and Ability to Attract Women

Introduction

Although known by different names, the image of the Alpha Male is one that has been around for countless generations. In more recent times, this image has been linked to success in all areas of life, resulting in an ever-growing number of books, classes, and videos on the subject. Unfortunately, many of these books and videos contain common misconceptions about the true nature of an Alpha Male. As such, they provide a false direction to those pursuing the Alpha lifestyle. They may provide only a handful of qualities and skills needed to become an Alpha Male, causing confusion and frustration. This book takes the time to dispel all the false images of a true Alpha Male, painting a clear and concise picture that will help you to better understand the goal you are trying to achieve. Furthermore, it will provide all the steps you need to take to begin eliminating the bad habits that have held you back your whole life, as well as the steps needed to develop the winning habits of an Alpha Male. By the time you finish reading this book, not only will you know what it truly means to be an Alpha Male, but you will have all the tools needed to transform yourself into one.

SECTION One: Self-Esteem

Chapter 1: Self-Esteem Explained

Self-esteem is the very foundation of a person's success. Without it, you can never hope to achieve anything worthwhile in life. Everything from finding the right job to forming happy and meaningful relationships relies on you having a strong, vibrant sense of self-esteem. Unfortunately, this is one area where most men struggle. In fact, most of the things that undermine their efforts at achieving high levels of self-esteem are those very things that pose as the ideals they are striving for. Images of men with ripped muscles, beautiful women, and bags of cash, although inspiring for a time, can eventually cause you to see yourself as less successful, less attractive, and ultimately less capable, leaving your self-esteem shattered. Seemingly ordinary habits can also lead to an erosion of your sense of self, causing you to lack the confidence and motivation needed to take your life to the levels you desire. Fortunately, once you recognize these false images and bad habits for what they are, you can eliminate the negative impact they have on your overall wellbeing. This chapter will explore some of the more common causes of low self-esteem, and the devastating effects they can have on your life. Additionally, it will provide a questionnaire enabling you to determine whether or not you suffer from low self-esteem. Finally, you will be shown four fundamental ways that are proven to develop the highest levels of self-esteem, levels reserved for the Alpha Male.

The True Nature of Self-Esteem

Before getting into the symptoms and causes of low self-esteem, a clear definition of self-esteem is needed. Most people confuse the terms "self-esteem" and "self-confidence", assuming that they are the same thing. While these two elements are closely linked, they are, in fact, two very distinct and different things. Self-confidence is the belief in your ability to be able to do a certain thing. If you have strong self-confidence, you will take more chances, believing that you can succeed. For example, you might approach a beautiful woman in a bar because you are highly confident in your ability to form a connection and start a relationship. , if you have low self-confidence, you will probably avoid such interaction as you believe your chances of failure far outweigh your chances of success.

Self-esteem, although related, is something different altogether. When you have high self-esteem, you have a high sense of self-worth. You believe that you are capable of achieving your goals, which is where self-confidence fits in. However, you also have a positive self-image, believing that your looks and overall style are things to be proud of, elements that will attract the right woman or help you in your effort to land the right job. Additionally, you will have a strong sense of self-worth in terms of your values, ethics, and other life fundamentals that give you a sense of pride in everything you do. Self-confidence is an integral part of self-esteem, but it is only a part and not the entirety.

The best way to understand the true nature of self-esteem as opposed to self-confidence is to reduce them to their simplest terms. Self-confidence can best be expressed by the statement, "I can." In contrast, self-esteem can best be expressed by the statement "I am." Self-confidence describes what you can do, while self-esteem describes who you are. Again, although self-confidence is a critical element of self-esteem, it is but one element. Many other elements go into creating the overall picture of self-esteem —the image you have of yourself and the value your life possesses.

Common Signs of Low Self-Esteem

Low self-esteem can come in many forms and can be caused by any number of factors. Fortunately, diagnosing the basic condition is relatively easy to do. Since low self-esteem is a generally negative condition, any and all negative habits or outlooks on life will usually point to it. Some of the more common signs that you might be struggling with low self-esteem include the following:

- **Image Shame:** This is when you are self-conscious about your overall appearance, either in terms of your body or in terms of your style. Sometimes this happens when you compare your current appearance with images of what is considered as the ideal male. These can be images of a muscular, tanned figure who looks more like a Greek statue than an actual human being, making the average male feel inferior when seeing their physique in the mirror. They can also come in the form of the well-groomed, flawless model wearing the latest fashions and attracting the most beautiful women imaginable. Such images will only serve to make the average person feel ashamed of their appearance compared to that of the airbrushed model in the image staring down at them.

- **Performance Anxiety:** This is when you feel stressed about not meeting other people's expectations. Sometimes this shows up in relationships where a man is worried about not satisfying his significant other. He may be afraid of not "wowing" his woman in bed, or not having enough money, style, or emotional experience to satisfy a woman's needs. Outside of relationships, performance anxiety affects millions of men in the workplace, the gym, and other areas in life where being the best seems somehow expected of everyone.

- **Isolation:** If you find that you avoid social encounters, preferring to remain alone, you might have low self-esteem. It is one thing to enjoy some quiet time in solitude, but it is quite another to avoid social gatherings because you don't feel good enough about yourself to be seen in public.

- **Self-Deprecation:** While the occasional self-deprecating joke can be a healthy way to ease tension with others, or to avoid appearing arrogant, making a habit of such jokes can point to a low sense of self-worth. This is especially true if those jokes cause discomfort rather than the laughs they are intended to generate.

- **A Lack of Desire for Self-Improvement:** This may seem a bit odd at first. After all, if you have high self-esteem, why would you want to improve yourself? However, the truth is that someone with a high sense of self-worth will always look for ways to become better, like a rich person always looking to make more money. The only reason you don't want to improve yourself is that you don't believe that you can.

- **Negative Expression:** Low self-esteem will show up in your language. Your body language will be negative, revealing uncertainty and anxiety. You will tend to say negative things, such as referring to goals as "impossible" or "unreasonable". You will never show enthusiasm when tackling something new or outside of your comfort zone.

While these are just a few of the more common signs of low self-esteem, they are easy to detect in your day-to-day life. The following questionnaire will help you to identify some of the more subtle ways that these causes may be presenting themselves in your life. If your answer is "yes" to most of the following questions, your self-esteem is low and needs to be fixed.

1. Do you avoid social interactions whenever possible, due to a sense of anxiety or shame?

2. Do you rely on using alcohol or some other substance to reduce anxiety and give you the courage to face your fears?

3. Do you often feel self-conscious about your physical appearance?

4. Is it hard for you to accept compliments from others?

5. Are you often overly apologetic, even for things that aren't your fault?

6. Do you avoid offering your opinion for fear that you will be ridiculed or found lacking intellectually?

7. Do you ignore personal grooming?

8. Are you surprised when people are happy to see you?

9. Do you constantly fish for compliments or validation?

10. Are you unable to make quick, specific decisions?

11. Are you suspicious of people who want to spend time with you?

12. Is your mind filled with doubt and memories of past failure?

13. Are you constantly comparing yourself to everyone around you?

14. Are you single or in a miserable relationship?

15. Are you unhappy with your job?

16. Are you unhappy in your life?

Common Causes of Low Self-Esteem

If you answered "yes" to most of the questions listed above, then you have low self-esteem. Hearing that may only make you feel worse at first, but the good news is that it probably isn't your fault at all. In fact, most people with low self-esteem have become that way as a result of their environment. For example, if you spend your time with negatively minded people, who constantly belittle one another as well as themselves, then you can't help but begin to feed into that negativity. After a while, your self-esteem will plummet, leaving you to take on the negative world view that those people share. Even if those people are your friends, the impact they have on your life can be devastating, making them, in fact, your worst enemies.

A person's upbringing can also impact their sense of self in a very real way. Parents who are abusive or neglectful will leave their children scarred for life, lacking the self-esteem that children of loving, positive parents have in abundance. This is because a person's self-image is largely learned. Therefore, if you grew up with your parents telling you that you are stupid, ugly, or a disappointment, then you will develop that belief. You will see yourself through their filters, focusing on your perceived faults, flaws, and shortcomings. In the end, these are the only things you will see, resulting in a complete lack of self-esteem.

Past experiences can also go a long way toward undermining your self-esteem. This goes hand-in-hand with self-confidence. If, for example, you try to lose ten pounds by going on a particular diet, but fail to achieve your goal, your self-confidence will take a hit. If you try two, three, or four other diets and continue to fall short of achieving your goals, you may be tempted to feel as though you simply aren't good enough to lose those ten pounds no matter what you do. Unfortunately, it only takes two or three failed attempts for most people before they give up, blaming themselves for their lack of success.

Finally, there is the issue of toxic stereotypes. Modern-day marketing has discovered that the best way to sell a product is to shame a person into buying it. This is why only the prettiest women model makeup or the latest fashions, while the most muscular or flawless men show off exercise equipment or the latest in men's fashions. In the end, it is the sense of feeling inferior to the models that make most people buy the clothes, the makeup, or the exercise machine. Unfortunately, none of those things ever transform the individual into the image in the picture, leaving them to give up, feeling inadequate, disappointed, and inferior.

Four Ways to Build Alpha Male Self-Esteem

If you have ever found yourself in any of these situations, take heart; you are not alone. Millions of men all around the world suffer from low self-esteem. Fortunately, none of the causes are without a cure. In fact, the path to recovery is often faster and easier than the path that led you to low self-esteem in the first place. The trick is to get to the heart of the problem rather than just trying to fix the symptoms. By curing the disease, you will eliminate the symptoms, leaving you with the high self-esteem that you need to achieve the success and happiness you both crave and deserve. The following are four ways to build Alpha Male self-esteem.

- **Develop Self-Awareness:** Ignoring problems usually doesn't do much toward solving them. The first step is to take the time to examine your feelings and to discover their causes. Address your fears, your doubts, and your regrets. Write them down so that you can begin to take control of them. Look them straight in the face and recognize the impact they have had on your life.

- **Address your Issues:** Once you have identified the issues that rob you of your self-esteem, the next step is to begin overcoming them. In the case of feeling ashamed of your appearance, recognize that you can change your appearance. Take the time to decide how you want to look, and then find every available resource that will help you achieve that goal. In the case of losing weight, find a gym, get a membership, and find a personal trainer or coach who can guide you so that you get the most from your effort. If it's a better job you want or better success at attracting women, figure out the areas you need to develop and begin pursuing those things. Find friends or life coaches who can offer insights and guidance, as well as an ear to bend when things don't go according to plan. In short, tackle your problems wholeheartedly.

- **Change your Story:** Once you have identified your issues and start to overcome them, you can begin to change your inner dialogue. Gone are the days of you not being good enough for success. Now that you are making strides in overcoming the things that robbed you of self-esteem, you can begin to feel better about yourself. Every victory, no matter how small, is a victory nonetheless, and it is worth celebrating. Even before you begin to lose weight, you can celebrate joining a gym, finding a coach, and developing a plan that will help you to achieve your goal. In short, you can celebrate taking charge of your life and changing course from failure to fulfilling your dreams.

- **Create the Big Picture:** Change comes in small, incremental measures at first. This is why it is vital to celebrate every win, no matter how small. However, you won't want to settle for small gains for long. Instead, you will want to create a bigger picture, the overall goal you hope to achieve with these small wins. For example, losing ten pounds might just be the beginning; you might want to start developing your muscles, getting some tone, and shaping a body that will give you pride when you go to the beach. Or you might want to change your style, buying clothes to show off your new shape, changing your hair cut for a more modern, fashionable look, or other similar changes. The important thing is to set your sights on the big prize, the ultimate goal. That will ensure that you stay motivated while remaining on the course that leads to your destination of life-changing success.

Chapter 2: Common Fears and Insecurities Men Have

To effectively fight any war, the first thing you need to do is to know your enemy. The fight for self-esteem is no exception to this rule. The only way you will be able to raise your levels of self-esteem to those of an Alpha Male is to identify the elements that serve to undermine your self-esteem in the first place. Only by removing and overcoming those obstacles will you be able to achieve your goal of self-transformation. Fortunately, the fears and insecurities that hinder your success are the same with which millions of other men all around the world struggle. So, they are well known, as are the methods for overcoming them. This chapter will deal with the fears and insecurities themselves, including how to identify them and what impact they have on your overall health and wellbeing. Only by knowing your own personal demons will you be able to choose the right methods of improvement from those offered in the rest of the book, thereby giving yourself the absolute best chance for success.

Inferior Physical Appearance

When it comes to self-esteem, few things are as vital as physical appearance. After all, your looks are more often than not the first thing anyone experiences about you. Even before they get to know your personality, your abilities, or your beliefs, they know what you look like. Although many would say not to judge a book by its cover, almost everyone does, and to a large degree. As a result, most men have serious fears and insecurities when it comes to their physical appearance.

The most commonly reported issue in this area comes in the form of the overall physique. Due to the increasingly sedentary nature of most lifestyles, it becomes harder and harder to keep unwanted weight off. Most men carry a few extra pounds around their waist, at the very least. While this isn't always a deal-breaker for most women, it is something that popular culture demonizes, especially within the advertising industries. Therefore, it is very common for men to feel self-conscious about their weight and their lack of muscle tone.

Another common fear concerning physical appearance is about one's hair. Baldness, although becoming more and more popular, is still seen as a non-Alpha Male trait. This is particularly true in the process leading up to baldness, namely the dreaded receding hairline. Men who experience thinning hair struggle with self-esteem, seeing it as a sign of their mortality and the fading of their masculinity. Other hair issues include chest or back hair. Some men feel that a lack of chest hair looks effeminate, while others are self-conscious about having too much body hair. There is no single measure by which the proper amount of body hair is defined, and this should not cause men to feel insecure.

A man's height can have a debilitating effect on his self-image. Tall men often feel exposed, as though they are the center of attention, whether or not they want to be. On the other end of the spectrum, short men often feel inferior, creating the well-known Napoleon Complex where short men have to prove themselves against their taller counterparts. Surprisingly enough, average-sized men can feel insecure due to their lack of distinction. Therefore, any and every height can affect a man in a very real and negative way, causing a problem that can't be readily resolved since you can't really change your height.

Inferior Performance

Even if you are lucky enough to feel perfectly happy with your physical appearance, including your height, your hair, and your weight, you still have to face the next obstacle, namely that of performance. The truth of the matter is that men are hardwired to be competitive. This can be traced back to primitive humans and the need to "win" a mate, either by brute force or by demonstrating better ability than other males present. Contests for females can be observed throughout nature, including birds singing and showing off bright plumage, primates challenging for dominance, or any number of species sparring to win the heart of the on-looking female. Although human culture and technology have advanced, human biology is still very much the way it was back in the days of our primitive cavemen ancestors. Therefore, the need to outperform every other male is alive and well in human males today.

Understandably, the main area where the need to outperform can be found is in the mating ritual itself. Countless men feel insecure when it comes to pleasing their woman in bed. This accounts for why porn is so popular. Numerous studies have shown that many men rely on porn for inspiration, hoping to learn tips and tricks to use to please their partners better. Most men still struggle with the fear that they aren't the best in that all-important arena. This is especially true in the case where their partner has had other lovers in the past. The fear of not matching up to former lovers can crush a man's spirit, and in a world where premarital sex is becoming the norm, such scenarios are becoming more and more common.

Another area where inferior performance is a very real fear is in providing for the family. Having a high paying, respectable job is the ideal for most men; when a man feels as though his job performance is inferior, he can struggle with self-esteem issues. Buying a bigger house, a flashier car, and having all the latest toys and gadgets can be either a way to overcome this fear or a way to show off when a man feels as though he is getting it done. However, such shows of vanity are more often than not an attempt to hide the deeper fears and insecurities of not always being the best when it comes to providing money and comfort for a man's family.

Performance fears can take many other forms, such as having to be the best at your job, a sport you play, or a hobby you enjoy. In the end, those things that are supposed to bring you joy and fulfillment can instead provide all sorts of opportunities to feel inferior and insecure. Needing to be the absolute best is a clear sign that you aren't secure in your natural ability but require the validation that being first can bring about. Likewise, needing to dominate at your job demonstrates a lack of security when it comes to your skills at work. In a society that is becoming faster paced and ever more competitive, the fear of not being good enough is becoming more and more widespread with each passing year.

Five Signs You Are Insecure

Sometimes fears and insecurities can be masked by behaviors that appear to be confident and strong. Such behaviors can leave the underlying causes of fear and insecurity unchecked, and the person's self-esteem continuing to be eaten away. Fortunately, the signs of insecurity are relatively easy to recognize. The following are five signs that you might be struggling with insecurity and low self-esteem:

- **Dishonesty:** No one likes a liar. When a person lies, they are covering up a truth they don't want to admit to or face. Therefore, if you find yourself lying to people regularly, it points to insecurity. This is particularly true if you lie about such things as your financial situation, your job, your skillset, or past experiences. If you have to invent stories to impress someone, you are insecure about your true self.

- **Being Needy:** The needier a person is, the less self-assured they are. After all, if you were a capable person with high self-esteem you wouldn't need other people to validate your life or take care of you. Neediness can come in many forms, including a sense of being helpless on your own, needing constant praise or validation from others, jealousy, rage, or other similarly unhealthy emotions that serve to undermine any relationship.

- **Extreme Introversion:** While being introverted in and of itself is not a sign of insecurity, extreme introversion is. The difference is in the nature of the introversion itself. If you prefer a quiet evening at home with your spouse or loved ones as opposed to going out on the town, that is not a bad thing. However, if you close yourself away from any and all human contact, that is a different situation altogether. Avoiding human contact is usually a sign of insecurity, and if you actively avoid social interaction, you need help rebuilding your sense of self-esteem.

- **Avoiding Eye Contact:** Social interaction is pretty much unavoidable, especially in the workplace, the grocery store, or any other place where you need to be regularly to sustain your day-to-day life. You can't hide insecurity when exposed to such social interactions. This is particularly true when it comes to eye contact. While a confident person will be able to maintain healthy and meaningful eye contact with someone they are talking to or listening to, someone struggling with insecurity will avoid such eye contact, much the way they would avoid social interaction altogether, given the choice.

- **Bullying Behavior:** The last sign of insecurity is one of the most misunderstood of them all, namely bullying behavior. It's natural to assume that a bully is someone confident of their capabilities; in fact, many aspects of bullying are wrongly attributed to the Alpha Male personality. The truth of the matter is that bullying behavior is a mask for serious insecurity. Most bullies are trying to keep others from noticing their low self-esteem; for that reason, they usually target people who personify their insecurities. Thus, if you pick on people who appear weak or who are different in one form or another, this is a sign that you are very insecure, and that your self-esteem needs a lot of work. Rather than being an Alpha Male, you are a poster child for fear and self-loathing, and have a complete lack of self-confidence.

The following checklist outlines the most common signs of insecurity. If you answer "yes" to most of the following, you need to keep reading, as your self-esteem needs to have a serious overhaul.

1. You wonder whether or not you are better than any lover from your significant other's past.

2. You lie about your finances, your job, or your past accomplishments.

3. You fixate on past successes, defining yourself by them.

4. You struggle to maintain eye contact with people.

5. You pick on or bully others, especially those you are secretly jealous of.

6. You rely on help from others for even the simplest of things.

7. You constantly compare yourself to others, feeling jealous and inferior as a result.

Chapter 3: Self-Doubt; Identifying and Thwarting Your Worst Enemy

When it comes to success, few things are as crucial as a strong sense of self-confidence. Skills, experience, and opportunities can all be learned and discovered. However, without self-confidence, none of those things will have the impact they otherwise could have. Unfortunately, many men lack the self-confidence that is required to achieve the success they crave. Instead, they are held back by a strong sense of self-doubt. The stronger a person's self-doubt, the harder it will be for them to achieve any real or significant success in their life.

Some symptoms of self-doubt are easy to identify, making it easy to face and overcome. However, some symptoms are more subtle, surviving in forms that are hard to detect, like cancer growing silently within. This chapter will discuss some of the most common symptoms of self-doubt, exploring the impact they can have on your life if they are allowed to exist unchecked. Additionally, this chapter will provide some easy and effective methods for overcoming self-doubt, thereby enabling you to achieve the success necessary to transform your life into that of an Alpha Male.

Common Signs of Self-Doubt

Many signs of self-doubt are obvious and easy to spot. If you constantly claim to be unable to do a certain thing, such as attract a woman or nail a job interview, then it is clear that you have serious doubts regarding your abilities in those areas. However, other symptoms of self-doubt can be harder to identify as they are disguised as rational concerns. For example, you might express self-doubt in such a way as to make the goal itself seem unreasonably hard. Instead of claiming to be bad at attracting a woman, you might use the excuse that the woman you are interested in hasn't shown any sign of being interested in you, or that she might not be looking for a relationship. Similarly, instead of putting the focus on your lack of confidence when trying to land the job of your dreams, you might focus on the fact that you don't have all the qualifications the position requires, or you might claim that your lack of experience stands against you. While these reasons may appear logical and rational, they are, in fact, symptoms of self-doubt. After all, when you have total confidence in your ability to overcome any obstacle, such issues won't be a deterrent. Instead, they will be a challenge you will happily accept.

Whether obvious or subtle, all forms of self-doubt serve to do one thing: undermine your chances of success. Therefore, you must take the time to assess your life and discover any self-doubt that might be lurking deep in your heart and mind. Identifying your self-doubts is the first step in your battle against those things that are keeping you from realizing your full potential. The following is a basic checklist outlining several of the more common signs of self-doubt. If you identify with most or all of these items, then self-doubt is a very real problem for you, one that needs to be addressed quickly and definitively.

1. You tend to hesitate about starting a new project, fearing you might not be able to complete it.

2. You lack the desire to step outside your comfort zone, even when the rewards are high.

3. You accept positions in life that are less than what you truly desire.

4. You agree with the negative things people say about you.

5. You fixate on your past failures, seeing them as signs of your inability to succeed.

6. It is hard for you to get motivated in the morning.

7. You envy the success of others.

8. You see your dreams as an escape rather than as a vision for what could be.

9. You feel self-conscious when working with others.

10. You constantly fear that you will lose what you have because of your inadequacies.

How Self-Doubt Affects You

In the end, if you recognized most or all of those elements as being a part of your life experience, you suffer from a high level of self-doubt. Now that you have recognized its existence, the next step is to understand how this self-doubt affects you. When you realize the damage that self-doubt is causing, it will serve as motivation for you to take a stand and eliminate self-doubt once and for all. The following are the three main negative impacts that self-doubt is having on your life:

- **A Lack of Drive:** Science has proven that life is all about energy. That said, there are two main charges of energy, positive and negative. When you have positive energy, you will experience positive effects, such as motivation, desire, and confidence. However, when you have negative energy, you will experience negative effects, such as a lack of drive. Thus, if you find that you lack inspiration, whether in terms of starting a new project, finding a new job, or just getting out of bed in the morning, you are suffering from the effects of self-doubt. This lack of drive can seem like a simple lack of energy at first, but what it really points to is a fear of failure. Only when self-doubt is removed can you restore your drive, thereby giving you the energy to chase your dreams.

- **A Lack of Fulfillment:** Self-doubt will often cause you to accept less than your dreams. This can come in the form of settling for a cheap car rather than the one you really want, a tiny house instead of the one you wish you had, or a job that pays the bills instead of one that brings meaning and fulfillment to your life.

- **A Lack of Success:** As mentioned before, self-confidence is one of the main ingredients in the recipe for success. That said, a lack of self-confidence will keep you from achieving success, because you will never take the first step in a journey you aren't confident of finishing. Therefore, you will take fewer and fewer chances in life, meaning that you achieve fewer and fewer successes. This lack of success is self-perpetuating. The fewer successes you have, the stronger your self-doubt will become, further hindering your chances of success down the road.

Easy and Effective Methods for Overcoming Self-Doubt

Fortunately, the methods for overcoming self-doubt are relatively simple, and easy to incorporate into your daily life. Furthermore, the methods presented in this chapter for overcoming self-doubt are highly effective, offering immediate results that will be noticeable to you and those close to you. The following are five of the easiest and most effective methods for overcoming self-doubt in all of its forms:

- **Eliminate Negative Influences:** If you take the time to ask yourself where your self-doubt comes from, you might be surprised at the answer. Often, self-doubt doesn't come from within, but from your environment. When you spend time surrounded by negative people, you will only hear negative thoughts and ideas. They will talk about how life is unfair, how any real success is impossible, and how trying to achieve your dreams will only end up in failure and despair. The more you hear this kind of talk is, the more you will begin to accept it as fact. Therefore, the first step to eliminating self-doubt is to eliminate its source, namely the negative people in your life.

- **Surround yourself with Positivity:** Once you remove the negative influences from your life, the next step is to replace them with positive influences. Try to surround yourself with successful people. Such people will have a more positive outlook on life, and that positivity will rub off on you, reprogramming your mind and eliminating the self-doubt that robs you of success. The more positivity you hear, the stronger your self-confidence will become.

- **Exercise:** One of the most ignored elements of self-doubt is its physiological causes. A lack of energy, whether physical, emotional, or mental, will often produce a sense of depression and lethargy, leading to a lack of motivation and, thus, a lack of success. Therefore, to break that cycle, you must increase your overall energy. The best way for this is to engage in some form of exercise that increases your heart and respiratory rates. Once the oxygen gets flowing through your body, your energy levels will increase, restoring confidence and inspiration.

- **Ignore your Past:** The most successful people are the ones who refuse to define themselves by their past. Instead, they focus on the present, taking every opportunity to improve their lives, becoming better and stronger every day. Focusing on the present will help you to let go of the past, especially any failures that could create self-doubt.

- **Turn Doubt into Desire:** Finally, recognize doubt for what it is. Sometimes self-doubt is a reaction to feeling you don't have the necessary skills or tools to tackle the task at hand. Rather than simply giving up, turn the doubt into the desire to acquire the skills or tools you need. You might need to ask for help, study up on a subject, or develop a new skill set. This is how growth works, so by turning doubt into desire you can grow as a result of every challenge you face. This will enable you to gain confidence as well as the experience you need to overcome every obstacle you face down the road.

Chapter 4: Body-Image Anxiety, and Four Ways to Overcome It

As discussed earlier, physical appearance can play a vital role when it comes to your sense of self-esteem. Body-image anxiety is on the rise among men, particularly in the West. Studies show that over the last twenty-four years the number of men with body-image anxiety has almost tripled, from fifteen percent of those surveyed to nearly forty-five percent. This means that as many as one in two men lack the confidence that a positive body image can provide, causing them higher levels of stress and lower levels of self-esteem. Fortunately, there are numerous proven techniques for eliminating body-image anxiety. This chapter will discuss the symptoms and effects of body-image anxiety, as well as the methods for overcoming it.

Common Forms of Body-image anxiety

Like any anxiety, body-image anxiety can take several different forms, each unique to the individual. The very attributes that some men envy can cause anxiety for those who possess them. This is because body image is all about perception. And, since each individual perceives their body differently, the anxiety they face will be different as well. Fortunately, the numerous types of body-image anxiety can be narrowed down to a few basic groups; the following are four of the most common types of body-image anxiety.

- **Weight:** Unsurprisingly, the most common of all body image anxieties is that of weight. As many as fifty percent of men feel that their weight undermines their value in the eyes of others. While extra weight and a large waist make up most of the numbers in terms of men who are self-conscious about their appearance, skinny men have also been found to suffer from body image-anxiety. Thus, it seems that the overall goal is to find that happy medium that represents strength and wellbeing. Anything else, one way or the other, results in anxiety and low self-esteem.

- **Height:** The second body image issue most men struggle with is height. Again, while short men envy the tall, most tall men suffer from their own anxieties. Stranger still, many men of average height feel that their height makes them blend in with the crowd, making them less impressive than their taller or even shorter counterparts. In the end, it seems that few men are satisfied with their height, wishing it were different in one direction or the other.

- **Muscle Tone:** This is the one area where the anxiety is easier to pinpoint, as it only goes in one direction. No man ever woke up and wished they had less muscle tone. Instead, all anxiety issues in this area come from men who feel inferior in terms of their muscular appearance. Although this might seem an easy issue to fix, one that requires little more than a gym membership, the truth of the matter is that body types are quite different, meaning that not all men can gain muscle tone simply by lifting weights.

- **Penis Size:** The final issue that causes many men body-image anxiety is that of penis size. In one survey, eighteen percent of men questioned said they were unhappy with their penis size. While the specific reasons for dissatisfaction varied, almost one in five men claimed to feel self-conscious about their penis size.

Common Effects of Body-image anxiety

Anxiety of any kind can lead to a lack of success as a result of avoiding opportunities because of one's low self-esteem.

Additionally, body-image anxiety can lead to several health issues, all stemming from an individual's urgent desire to change their physical appearance. Some of the more common effects of body-image anxiety include:

- **Isolation:** Any time a man feels anxious about his physical appearance, he is more likely to avoid social contact. Isolation can lead to loneliness, depression, and an ever-growing sense of self-loathing. In more extreme cases, this can lead to thoughts and even acts of self-harm or suicide.

- **Low Self-Esteem:** As with any anxiety, self-esteem is significantly impacted when a man is self-conscious about his body image. He may begin to associate his body image with failures he experiences in life, including failed relationships, loss of employment, or a general sense of dissatisfaction with life. Since some body-image issues are hard to change, this can cause a person to feel helpless in terms of ever hoping to improve their life in any significant way.

- **Health Issues:** When a person struggles to gain or lose weight, they will often turn to supplements for help. Unfortunately, this can lead to health issues, especially when the supplements are not taken as directed, or when they are combined with others in an attempt to speed up the process. Abuse of diet pills, muscle-building compounds, and the like can lead to serious health issues, including death. Any sudden and unnatural increase or decrease in weight can impact a person's organs, causing such things as heart disease, kidney failure, and even diabetes.

- **Eating Disorders:** An all too common consequence of body-image anxiety is eating disorders. These can range from starvation diets in an attempt to lose weight to overeating in an attempt to gain weight. If a man is unable to lose weight, he may resign himself to remaining overweight, thereby becoming depressed and turning to food for comfort. Not only will this make his body-image anxiety worse, but it will also lead to potential health issues as well as depression.

Common Benefits of a Positive Body Image

When a man has a positive sense of his body image, things are quite different in terms of his overall health and wellbeing. The better a man feels about his appearance, the better he feels about himself all around. This leads to a stronger sense of self-esteem, which leads to a greater amount of self-confidence, which leads to more success in life overall. Some of the common benefits of a positive body image include:

- **Higher Levels of Self-Esteem:** When a person feels good about how they look, it increases their sense of self-worth, which inspires greater self-confidence. This translates into a better social life, better relationships with women, and even a greater chance of being satisfied in their job. The confidence that comes from feeling good about how you look translates into success in virtually every area of your life.

- **Better Health:** Another common benefit of a positive body image is better health. In a way, this can be likened to how a man treats his car. If he hates his car, the chances are he won't invest the time or energy keeping it clean and waxed and properly maintained. If he loves his car, he will keep it clean and shiny, putting the best gas in the tank and sparing no expense on parts. This is precisely how a man will treat his body. When he loves his body, he will exercise more, eat better foods, and take more time grooming. All of this increases his appearance and health, which in turn increases his confidence and overall sense of self.

Four Ways to Overcome Body-Image Anxiety for Good

While some aspects of body image are controllable, such as your appearance in terms of grooming or your general weight, others are less changeable, such as your height. Fortunately, changing your body image has more to do with your perception than it does with your actual body. You can feel good about yourself without altering your height, weight, or even muscle tone. The trick is to eliminate the negative narrative and replace it with a sense of self-worth that makes you feel good about yourself once again. The following are four ways to overcome body-image anxiety for good:

- **Eliminate the Myth of "Perfection":** One of the chief reasons people, both men, and women, develop body-image anxiety is that they feed into a notion of how their body is supposed to look. Posters, TV ads, and magazines relentlessly bombard people with images of the ideal body, making them feel inferior. The easiest way to overcome this effect is to stop seeing those images as anything but the lie they are. Perfection is a myth, pure and simple. And the images in those ads are usually airbrushed and enhanced to achieve visual perfection, anyway, meaning that they are a total lie aimed at getting you to buy a product or membership.
- **Play to your Strengths:** Sure, you might wish you were taller, or shorter, or had more hair or less hair. You might point to half a dozen things you wish were different about your appearance. That doesn't mean there aren't at least half a dozen things to be proud of. No one would ever criticize a pitcher on a baseball team for his low batting average. Nor would they expect the first baseman to get up on the mound and strike out the next batter. In baseball, as in any sport, each player focuses on their strengths to be their best. That is the trick to improving your body image. Find your best physical features and enhance them. You might have great hair, eyes, or skin. Draw attention to these things by making them what people see first. Choose clothes that make you look good, thereby giving you greater confidence. Don't focus on what you can't change; instead, focus on what works and make the most of those things.
- **Take Charge of Your Health:** Even if you can't lose or gain the exact amount of weight you want, that doesn't mean you should give up altogether. Living a healthier life will be better, no matter what. When you take the time to exercise and eat right, your body

image will improve. Again, it's not about being perfect; it's about being the perfect you. As you take better care of your body, your body will perform better, and that will increase your body image exponentially.

- **Stop Comparing Yourself to Others:** Finally, you must stop comparing yourself to others. Sure, there will be other men who have better muscle tone, are the right height, the right shape, and whatever. Good for them. Don't compare yourself to them, though. Instead, recognize that your body is unique. Appreciate what you have and make the most of it. That is the key to self-esteem. It's not about being better than everyone else; it's about being the best that you can be.

Chapter 5: Five Ways to Boost Your Self-Esteem NOW

As already mentioned, self-esteem is the foundation on which any success is built. No matter what type of success you crave, your chances of success are in direct proportion to your self-esteem. When your sense of self-worth is high, your chances of realizing your ambitions will also be high; when your sense of self-esteem is low, your chances of successfully turning dreams into reality will be equally low. Therefore, before you take any action toward achieving your life goals, you must start building your sense of self-esteem. The process of building self-esteem is a gradual one, much like building muscle tone or losing weight. Fortunately, as long as you are willing to put in a little time and effort every day, the road to building high levels of self-esteem will be an easy one to travel. This chapter will discuss five of the most effective methods for giving your self-esteem the boost it so desperately needs. Once you implement these five methods into your daily routine, you will begin to notice a stronger sense of self-worth, which will increase your sense of self-confidence, thereby enabling you to tackle any challenge or pursue any goal imaginable with the best chances of success.

Live Healthy

The first thing to realize is that your mental health and wellbeing are directly connected to your physical health and wellbeing. In fact, a person's weight can often tell you the exact condition of their mind. When a person is overweight and unhealthy, their mind will be sluggish, often full of doubt and generally lacking the self-esteem necessary for achieving their life goals and ambitions. However, when a person is in good physical shape, their mind will tend to be sharper, and their self-esteem will be stronger, providing them with the confidence and peace of mind needed to tackle any challenge that comes their way effectively, thus placing them in charge of their life. Therefore, the first step toward developing high self-esteem is to get your physical health and wellbeing sorted out.

Food plays a bigger role in an individual's mental wellbeing than most people realize. Just as unhealthy foods can add unwanted pounds to your waistline, as well as clogging your arteries and creating all sorts of conditions that undermine your physical health, so too, they can have the very same impact on your mental health. Food is fuel, and your mind needs fuel to function just as much as your body does. Thus, when your diet consists of junk fuel, not only will your body suffer, but your mind will suffer as well. Depression, sluggish thinking, and an overall negative mindset go hand in hand with a diet filled with unhealthy foods. Therefore, the first thing you need to do is to replace processed foods with natural foods such as fruit and vegetables.

Additionally, make sure you eat foods rich in minerals and protein, such as eggs, fresh fish, and chicken. Get rid of sugary drinks such as soda and start drinking more water. Milk is another good choice as it contains plenty of vitamins and nutrients and has been proven to be one of the best liquids for keeping your body hydrated.

The next step to developing a healthy lifestyle is to exercise regularly. This doesn't necessarily mean you have to go out and get a gym membership today; exercise can be done at home with little to no extra gear required. Yoga, for example, is a perfect regimen to improve your heart and respiratory rates. As these rates improve, so too will your mental health and wellbeing. This will give you better clarity of mind, better memory, and an overall healthier sense of self-worth. Running is another good exercise that can boost your blood flow, thereby improving your mental performance as well as your sense of self-esteem. Starting with these exercises will get you moving in the right direction, increasing your sense of accomplishment as well as your motivation to take things to the next level.

Develop Mindfulness

The second method for giving your self-esteem an immediate boost is to develop mindfulness. This can tend to sound very Zen, and it's true that the Zen tradition is heavily steeped in mindfulness. However, you don't have to be spiritual or in search of meaning to achieve the mindfulness that you need for higher levels of self-esteem. Instead, you simply have to take the time to better understand your mind and how it works.

The best way to do this is to take time every day to sit down and be alone with your thoughts. Explore your mind, seeing and hearing all the thoughts, ideas, images, and sounds that it contains. As soon as you see an image, hear a thought, or grasp an idea, take the time to consider its meaning carefully. Where did it come from? Is it positive or negative? Any negative thought or image needs to be addressed right away as those can significantly undermine your self-esteem. Sometimes these will be the result of negative words spoken by others. Someone may have told you that a plan or idea is impossible, or that you don't have what it takes to accomplish your goals. Such thoughts need to be seen for what they are, namely the negativity of others. Once you realize that they don't actually belong to your mind, you can release them and the negativity they contain. What are left are the hopes, ambitions, and positive thoughts that will boost your self-esteem, thereby giving you the confidence necessary to achieve your goals.

Improve Your Image

The next step toward developing high levels of self-esteem is to improve your image. Although your image is something you don't see from within, the more confident you are in your appearance, the higher your sense of self-esteem will be. Therefore, this is an absolutely vital element to developing the highest levels of self-esteem, those fit for an Alpha Male.

The first area to tackle is your wardrobe. If your closet is full of uninspiring clothes, then not only will your image fail to impress others, it will fail to create high levels of self-esteem. Therefore, take the time to go through your closet and weed out all the clothes that are mediocre in style and appearance. Once you have made the space, you can go shopping for the clothes that will give your appearance the boost it needs. While loose-fitting clothes are good for sitting on the sofa, they aren't good for anything else. Therefore, fill your closet with clothes that fit well. A tailor-made shirt can make all the difference when it comes to making that all-important first impression. Pants that are the right length and fit well will help you not only look like the proverbial million dollars; they will help you feel that way, especially when you see people taking notice of you.

The next area to tackle is grooming. Always take the time to keep your fingernails and toenails neatly trimmed. Although you might be the only one to see your toes, by taking the time and effort to keep them trimmed, you are sending the message that you are worth the extra attention, and this will help boost your self-esteem. Additionally, taking the extra time and effort to make your hair look its best is vital. If you have a ten-dollar haircut you are telling yourself and everyone else that you are only worth ten dollars. However, when you spend the cash on a haircut that is tailor-made to your face, as well as the product to keep it looking its best, you are telling the world that you are worth the extra time and expense. This will make all the difference in how you feel when you step through the door into the world outside.

Manage Your Goals

When it comes to keeping your self-esteem strong and healthy, few things are as vital as a sense of accomplishment. If you struggle to achieve your goals or to make measurable progress toward fulfilling your dreams, then your self-esteem will suffer. However, when you achieve goals daily and can track your progress toward realizing the final goals, then your self-esteem will remain strong and vibrant. Fortunately, this comes down to one simple concept, that of managing your goals.

The first step toward effective goal management is to break down large goals into smaller, more achievable ones. This can keep you from feeling overwhelmed by larger projects or tasks that will take a long time to accomplish fully. Instead of approaching a big task as a single goal, you should break it down into numerous, smaller goals. This will allow you to measure the progress you are making, as well as giving you a sense of accomplishment along the way. Furthermore, as you accomplish each smaller goal, you will maintain your motivation for getting the overall project completed, thereby keeping your self-confidence high every step of the way.

Another way to manage your goals is to keep a tight schedule. Don't let yourself fall into the trap of saying that you will get to a project when you have more time. Break down large projects into smaller, more manageable tasks and give yourself realistic deadlines for those tasks. Take the time to write down your goals daily, listing out the things you want to achieve every day. If you find you are falling behind schedule, either increase your effort or reduce your workload. The important thing is to set achievable goals and to give yourself a realistic timeframe in which to get them done. This will increase your productivity, which in turn will increase your sense of self-esteem.

Be Sociable

Finally, to nurture a healthy sense of self-esteem, you must become sociable. While time alone can be a good and healthy thing, too much time alone can lead to feelings of isolation. One of the biggest problems with isolation is that it robs you of positive interactions with other people. Such interactions are critical to build and maintain high levels of self-esteem. Therefore, you must spend time with other people who can provide the positive energy and experiences needed to improve your sense of self-worth.

Spending time with the wrong people, however, can harm your self-esteem. People who are negative in their approach to life, always pointing out the bad things, gossiping about others, or just spending all their time talking about failure should be avoided at all costs. It would be better to be alone than to be in the company of negatively minded people. When you spend time with positive people, those who talk about their dreams and how they are planning to achieve them, or who offer advice and support for you in your efforts to turn your dreams into reality, then you will gain the inspiration and motivation that their positivity creates. Therefore, make sure to spend time, not just with people but with the right people.

SECTION Two: Alpha Male Habits

Chapter 6: The Alpha Male Profile

To become an Alpha Male, the first thing you need to do is understand exactly what an Alpha Male is. Unfortunately, many of the common notions regarding the true nature of an Alpha Male are incorrect and misleading. Most images of Alphas involve men with chiseled abs and thick biceps. Although physical strength can be significant, it is not a defining aspect of what being an Alpha Male is all about.

Furthermore, many still believe that Alpha Males have to be aggressive and intimidating. Not only is this untrue, but it is also actually the opposite of what it means to be an Alpha. Therefore, before getting into the nuts and bolts of how to develop the heart and mind of an Alpha Male, it is vital to define what this term truly means. This chapter will reveal the profile of an Alpha Male, exploring such things as the behavior, mindset, and lifestyle that are necessary for achieving this coveted title. Furthermore, it will reveal some of the benefits that come from being an Alpha Male, benefits that make the effort absolutely worthwhile.

The Language of Alphas

The first thing that separates Alpha Males from all others is the language they speak. This isn't about whether you speak English, Japanese or French; it is a different language, one that reveals the heart and mind of the Alpha Male. This language has its own tone, structure, and content, and when it is spoken, it commands the attention and respect of all who hear it.

The tone of the Alpha Male language is always confident. As such, it is neither submissive nor overbearing. A big misconception is that as an Alpha, you must always speak in a raised voice, using your proverbial "outside" voice even when indoors. This isn't the true tone of an Alpha. Instead, an Alpha Male speaks in an authoritative tone, one that is strong without being overbearing, and caring without being weak. It is neither too fast nor too slow, but deliberate and measured in its rhythm. When an Alpha Male speaks, others listen because they want to, not because they are forced to. This is one way in which an Alpha Male commands the respect of those around him.

The structure of the Alpha Male language is positive. Rather than being filled with uncertainty, it is direct and assertive. An Alpha Male will never ramble; instead, they will get straight to the point as quickly as possible. This doesn't mean that you have to be blunt and merciless in what you say. Instead, it means that you don't beat around the bush. If you have a point to make, make it. Don't sugar-coat it, and don't beat people over the head with it. In short, it comes down to integrity. An Alpha Male's words are always straight and true. They serve to convey his thoughts and feelings, nothing more, nothing less.

Finally, there is the content of the Alpha Male language. This is where positivity and confidence come into play. An Alpha Male will never belittle anyone else, even if they disagree with that person. Instead, they will always focus on the merits of their own convictions, allowing others to make up their own minds. Furthermore, their words will always be positive, demonstrating the Alpha's confidence and motivation regarding the situation at hand. There is no place for negativity, bullying, or surrender in the language of an Alpha Male. Instead, their words will be full of hope, assurance, and inspiration.

They will always focus on the solution rather than the problem, demonstrating the fact that they are truly in charge of the situation.

Being Goal Oriented

Another vital aspect of the Alpha Male profile is that of being goal oriented. Everyone has dreams of one sort or another, including dreams of getting rich, finding the perfect job, or marrying the perfect woman. However, where most people fall short is in turning those dreams into reality. This is where goals are all-important. Goals are the tools with which a person can turn their dreams into reality. Without goals, dreams will never be realized, leaving the individual to live a life of mediocrity. Alphas are determined to realize their dreams, and they know that the only way to achieve that is to be goal oriented.

One way that an Alpha Male is goal oriented is how they take the time to carefully consider what has to happen to turn their dreams into reality. Once they have a dream, they begin planning how to achieve that dream. Creating goals to move them in the right direction is what an Alpha Male will do as soon as they have a clear idea of what their dream is. Rather than just being dreamers, Alpha Males are doers as well. They are the complete package. Not only can they imagine how their life can be better, they also establish the goals necessary to turn that vision into reality.

Another way that Alpha Males are goal-oriented is that they remain focused on their goals at all times. This is a sign of immeasurable discipline, especially in a world filled with distractions of all shapes and sizes. While others will end their day with hours of TV, games, or other distractions, Alpha Males will use that time to further their ambitions. Instead of wasting time, they invest their time, reaping the benefits of fulfilling their dreams. While Alpha Males might appear as workaholics at times, the truth is that they are simply unwilling to rest until their goals are achieved, and their lives transformed into their dreams.

Being A Leader

The Alpha Male is the top dog, the one in charge, the one that everyone else follows. Therefore, as an Alpha Male, you must be a leader.

There are many qualities to leadership, qualities that not only make a true leader stand out from the crowd but that serve to engender trust, confidence, and respect in those around them. One of the most important of all leadership qualities is that of integrity. Not only must an Alpha Male speak the truth at all times, but they must also stay true to their principles. This means that they must always make the right choice, even when that choice might be the hardest one to make. Rather than giving in to pressure from peers or even pressure from superiors, an Alpha Male will always stay true to his personal beliefs. An Alpha Male will run the risk of being fired from his job or ostracized by his friends and family rather than doing something that goes against his core values. This unwavering sense of right is what is at the very heart of a true Alpha Male.

Another vital element of being a leader is the ability to connect to others. This includes those above you, around you, and in your charge. A true Alpha Male will listen to what others have to say, taking their opinions seriously even if he doesn't agree with them. He recognizes that to get others to listen to him, he must listen to them as well. Making even the lowest person on the totem pole feel important is a trait of an Alpha Male. This means that the bullying, overbearing image of Alpha Males that is so prevalent today is about as far from the truth as you could get. A real Alpha doesn't have to threaten or bully people into submission; instead, they can assert their authority simply by showing true strength of character.

Finally, to be a good leader, you must be able to lead by example. Just because someone is in charge doesn't mean they are a good leader. A good way to tell the difference is to see whether or not the person in charge holds themselves to the same standards as they hold everyone else. Inept leaders will often use the phrase, "Do as I say, not as I do." This demonstrates a total weakness of character since it means the leader is incapable of maintaining the standards they expect of others.

In contrast, an Alpha Male will hold themselves to even higher standards than those around them. This means that they will lead by example, always putting forth a strong work ethic, a willingness to learn new skills, and the ability to adapt to changing situations. In short, they will never expect others to do what they are not willing or able to do themselves.

Benefits of Being an Alpha Male

The qualities of an Alpha Male discussed above are far from a complete list. Even so, they represent some of the most demanding and disciplined aspects a person could ever hope to achieve. This often leads to questions of whether or not the effort is worthwhile. After all, there had better be something at the end of the race to make the race worth running. Fortunately, there are many benefits to being an Alpha Male. In fact, the benefits are so numerous and so significant that they make every effort required for becoming an Alpha Male almost seem minimal in comparison.

One such benefit of being an Alpha Male is the sense of being your own person. Most people resign themselves to being a product of their environment or their opportunities. This means that they live a life largely decided for them by others. In contrast, an Alpha Male never defines himself or his potential by his surroundings. Instead, he determines his own life by following his ambitions, no matter where they may lead. This means that as an Alpha, you will never be a victim again. Your fate won't be decided by the family you were born into, or the opportunities others offer. Instead, your fate will be determined by your ambitions and your ability to realize those ambitions.

Another benefit of being an Alpha Male is the choices at your disposal. The more average a person is, the more average their choices are. Someone with mediocre ambitions will only ever achieve mediocre success. The jobs available to them will be limited in terms of fulfillment and financial gain. The women who are in "their league" will be mediocre, promising a future of modest happiness. While these can be enough for many, it is hardly the stuff dreams are made of. This is where being an Alpha Male can make all the difference. Once you develop and integrate Alpha qualities into your life, you will find your opportunities increase exponentially. Better jobs are within reach, higher income levels are there for the taking, and the woman of your dreams will want to share her life with you as she recognizes the Alpha Male within you.

Finally, when you are an Alpha Male, your perspective on life changes dramatically. While most people wake up day after day wondering what obstacles they will face in the day to come, as an Alpha Male you will wonder what opportunities await you in the day ahead. This makes every day a wonderful adventure, full of unlimited potential. Rather than dreading the future, you will eagerly anticipate it. The reason for this is that you know your ability to make things happen, so each day is an opportunity for you to make yet another dream come true. Thus, instead of life being something to be endured or tolerated, it becomes something to get excited about. Every day will be a tool that you use to turn your dreams into reality. As an Alpha Male, life's challenges don't dictate your life to you, but allow you to live it.

Chapter 7: Why Women Prefer Alphas

Although it stands to reason that women would prefer Alpha Males over any other type, there can still be a bit of confusion in this area. After all, there are plenty of books and articles devoted to the subject of women being attracted to gentle, caring men who aren't afraid to show their emotional side. This has led to many men choosing to pursue a Beta Male lifestyle in hopes of being more attractive to women. Unfortunately for them, the notion of women preferring Beta Males is completely misguided. Half of the reason is that many of the Alpha-Male traits women claim to be turned off by aren't true qualities of the Alpha Male at all. In fact, they are qualities an Alpha Male would reject. The other half of the reason is that while women want to be able to share a tender, emotional moment with their man, they don't want to have to baby him, as is often the case with Beta Males.

The reasons why women prefer Alpha Males are very simple and straightforward. This chapter will reveal several of those reasons, giving you the inside scoop on why you will attract more women when you develop your Alpha Male lifestyle.

The Primal Mind

When discussing the reasons why women prefer Alpha Males, one of the first things to consider is the biology of the situation.

Humans are a species of mammals, hardwired in many ways the same as any other species in nature. This means that the emotions and impulses that drive us are primal, the very same ones that drove our cave-dwelling ancestors to make the same sorts of choices that we make today. In this light, it becomes obvious why a woman would prefer to share her life with an Alpha Male.

For one thing, Alpha Males are stronger. Again, this isn't necessarily about muscles or martial arts abilities; rather, it's about strength of character. An Alpha Male has the confidence and drive needed to achieve his goals. Therefore, he is seen as stronger than those who are timid or who lack motivation. Although what constitutes strength in the Alpha Male has evolved over the millennia, the natural attraction to strength has not, meaning that women are instinctively drawn to Alpha Males more so than to any other type.

Although the ability to achieve goals can enable an Alpha Male to achieve success and fame, the true significance of this ability is that the Alpha Male can provide security for himself and his family. This is another way in which the primal mind can be seen at work. What a woman craves is the certainty that she will always have a comfortable home, plenty of food, and all of her needs met. Since an Alpha Male is the epitome of success, both in the workplace as well as in other environments, such security is always guaranteed. Thus, just as the prehistoric woman was attracted to the male who could build a solid shelter and successfully hunt for food, so too, the modern woman is attracted to the man who can satisfy her basic needs.

Finally, there is the matter of pride. While it's likely that Alpha Males in prehistoric times would compete in feats of strength to get their position, modern-day Alphas don't have to rely on such acts any longer. Instead, having a prestigious job, a nice house, and a strong bank account provide the same bragging rights as did knocking the other males to the ground back in the day. Although such things may be seen as shallow and materialistic by some, the fact is that they all point to the financial security that triggers that primal drive. Not only is it a primal drive in Alpha Males to achieve such success, but it is also a primal drive in females to be attracted to it. No woman was ever put off by a large bank account, a big house, or a lifestyle that was too good. Instead, they are put off by the arrogance, misogyny, and abusive behavior of a Beta Male who has those things. The security and happiness that such things provide is always attractive to any woman, both ancient and modern.

Alpha Attributes That Women Love

If you haven't yet achieved the fortune that will attract a woman, never fear. Many Alpha Male attributes will attract a woman regardless of your bank account or the car you drive. However, those attributes should serve to drive you to achieve success in other areas, thereby proving that you can provide the security and happiness every woman wants.

One such attribute is that of confidence. No matter what situation an Alpha Male finds himself in, one certain thing is that he will always be confident of achieving success. Even if his life has been turned upside down by forces beyond his control, rather than mourning his losses and dreading the future, a true Alpha Male will see his condition as an opportunity to build a fresh life, one that is even better than the one he lost.

Such confidence doesn't lead to arrogance, however. Instead, it leads to cooperation and support on a level that is unmistakable. Men who sing their own praises, often at the expense of belittling others, aren't showing confidence or pride; they are showing a need for validation, something that reflects insecurity and anxiety. Alpha Males will share their confidence with others, offering support, guidance, and even help to others who are struggling to achieve their goals. Such confidence brings with it a sense of compassion that resonates with women. This is one of those areas of confusion regarding true Alpha Male qualities. Showing compassion isn't a Beta Male trait, rather it is a trait of someone who isn't afraid of being shown up and who craves success, both for himself as well as for those around him. In short, compassion is very much a trait of an Alpha Male.

Another Alpha Male trait that draws in women is that of dominance. Herein is another example of misunderstanding the true nature of the Alpha-Male mindset. Dominance doesn't mean that you rise to the top by stepping on those around you. Instead, it is a matter of energy. When you crave success like an Alpha Male, you put in your best performance every time you take on a challenge. This can be in any area at all, including projects at work, projects at home, or even a fun day out with friends and loved ones. A simple game of darts, for example, will bring out the competitive nature of an Alpha Male. Even though it's just a game, one that won't change anyone's life in any way, shape, or form, an Alpha Male will put every effort into winning. His energy and commitment will make him stand out, dominating those around him. The best part is that even if he doesn't win, not only will his exceptional efforts be recognized, his graciousness in defeat will also make him stand out head and shoulders above the rest. It's not that he enjoys losing as such. Rather, it shows that he is strong enough to share in another person's success.

What Alpha Males Bring to a Relationship

While a show of financial security and reliable attributes will go a long way to attracting a woman, these may not prove enough to keep her by your side once you win her over. To achieve that goal, the goal of keeping a woman for the long term, you need to master the traits that make a relationship work. Fortunately, the same traits that ensure an Alpha Male success in other areas of life will also ensure success in the area of long-term relationships. Therefore, while Beta Males will struggle to keep a woman interested, Alphas will keep a woman by their side for as long as they choose.

One of the most important Alpha Male qualities when it comes to making a relationship work is that of being direct. While women might like a bit of mystery, they don't like to play games when it comes to starting a relationship. A mistake most men make is that they say whatever they think a woman wants to hear to get their foot in the proverbial door. Unfortunately, as time progresses, those statements are seen as deceptions, leading to conflict and failed relationships. In contrast, Alpha Males are always honest, telling a woman the truth about everything from the start. Although this truth may not be ideal, such as the Alpha Male not liking dogs while the woman is a dog lover, at least she will know upfront that there are challenges to be met. This creates trust and respect, qualities that are the very foundation of every successful and long-lasting relationship.

Another way in which the mindset of an Alpha Male is beneficial in a relationship is that it reduces and even eliminates stress on the part of the woman. One of the main causes of stress in a relationship is uncertainty. If a woman is unsure of how the man feels or what he is thinking, she can create all kinds of negative scenarios in her mind that cause untold stress and anxiety. An Alpha Male will always be direct with his thoughts and feelings, removing any uncertainty and the stress and anxiety such uncertainty can cause. This also prevents a woman from feeling as though she is wasting her time. Instead of putting vast amounts of time and effort into an uncertain relationship, she will know whether the relationship has a future by the things the Alpha Male says and does.

Finally, the confidence of an Alpha Male will go a long way toward creating a healthy and vibrant relationship on all levels. One thing that this confidence will do is enable an Alpha to open up to his partner. This prevents her from feeling shut out, as is the case with so many "macho" men who are, in fact, Beta in nature. Since an Alpha is unafraid of rejection, he will be completely willing to share his feelings on any matter. This is the tender side of a man that is often wrongly associated with Beta Males.

This confidence will also enable an Alpha to step out of his comfort zone. There will be a time in any relationship where the woman wants to do something that the man simply does not want to do. While Betas will either refuse to participate or find excuses that allow them to avoid the issue, Alphas will gladly, if reluctantly, indulge their partner in an activity that would bring other men to their knees. Going to a chick flick, for example, is something that an Alpha might not want to do, but he will gladly do it to make his woman happy. He won't be concerned about who sees him entering or leaving the theater, and he won't have to bring a chain saw to prove he is still a man. He will accompany his lady with pride and confidence, making him stand out in a way most men only ever dream of.

Why You Should Go the Alpha Way

In the end, if you want to both attract and keep the woman of your dreams, there is only one way to go; the way of the Alpha Male. Again, this isn't about getting ripped with muscles to impress, nor is it about being tough and macho. The trick is to be a true Alpha, someone full of confidence and integrity, qualities that will enable you to please any woman for any length of time. As well as being qualities that benefit the woman, the Alpha qualities of confidence and integrity will also keep you happy as well.

One way that confidence can make you happy in terms of a relationship is that it will keep you from staying in a relationship that makes you miserable. There are times when the woman of your dreams may turn out to actually be the stuff of nightmares. If you lack the confidence to find another, better relationship, you may resign yourself to being miserable in lieu of being alone. However, when you possess the confidence of an Alpha Male, you know that you not only deserve better but that you are capable of finding better. This will allow you to leave a toxic relationship before it can negatively affect your life.

Another way that confidence will benefit you is that you will never be afraid of losing the woman of your dreams to another man. Sometimes even a Beta Male can do the right things and say the right words to win the prize. However, such a prize will only cause him misery down the road as he will always be jealous and suspicious of any other man. When you have the confidence of an Alpha Male, you will feel secure in the fact that the woman of your dreams will never leave your side. No man will be able to compete with you and win her affections. This will make every day with her one to be celebrated, not feared.

Chapter 8: Alpha Male Habit #1: Confidence

The key to developing any kind of lifestyle is to develop the right habits. This is evident even in terms of bad lifestyles, where habits such as eating fast food and not getting exercise lead to poor health, low self-esteem, and a mediocre life at best. In contrast, when you create positive, strong habits, you will create a positive and strong lifestyle. This applies to even the strongest and most positive of lifestyles, namely that of the Alpha Male. Since confidence is the foundation on which the Alpha Male lifestyle is built, the first habit you need to form is that of practicing confidence. This chapter will discuss the things to avoid when creating this habit, such as the many false faces of confidence that are commonly mistaken as Alpha Male qualities. Additionally, you will be given specific actions to take daily that will make confidence a natural part of your behavior. Finally, some of the benefits of having confidence in your life will be presented, giving you extra motivation for getting started on developing your Alpha Male lifestyle.

False Faces of Confidence

It may seem repetitive to keep referring to the qualities most people mistakenly associate with being an Alpha Male, but the truth of the matter is that these qualities can be devastating to anyone who is trying to develop a true Alpha Male lifestyle. Therefore, before you begin learning the true signs of confidence and the steps needed to develop them, it is vital that you recognize the false faces of confidence so that you can avoid them at all costs. The following are some of the most common false faces of confidence:

- **Bullying People:** The behavior of a bully may appear as confident, but you should recognize that it is actually quite cowardly, because a bully invariably picks on someone they think weaker than themselves.

- **Bragging:** While bragging may appear confident, it is, in fact, a sign that a person needs validation. Someone who is truly confident won't have to put themselves in the spotlight the way a braggart does. Instead, they are confident of their abilities regardless of what others may say. They are happy to remain silent about their successes; they never have to seek praise or recognition.

- **Gossiping:** Like bullying, gossiping is when one person denigrates another, although in this case, it's behind their back. No person with self-confidence would engage in this behavior; putting other people down to look good is just another form of cowardice.

- **Habits of Insecure People**

In addition to false faces of confidence, some habits must absolutely be avoided to build an Alpha Male lifestyle. These habits are those caused by a lack of self-esteem and self-confidence. While some may seem harmless enough, if allowed to continue, they will undermine your efforts at creating the life of your dreams. Some common habits of insecure people include the following:

- **Needing Constant Validation:** One of the most tell-tale signs of insecurity is a constant need for validation. If you constantly seek approval, recognition, or the proverbial pat on the back, you lack the self-esteem of an Alpha Male. Only when you quit this habit can you begin to form those that will give you the confidence you desire.

- **Lack of Grooming:** One thing that builds confidence is taking care of your physical appearance. Thus, when you stop taking care of such things as your hair, skin, and other basic elements, you demonstrate a low sense of self-esteem. Never let yourself fall into the habit of poor personal grooming.

- **Apathy:** When someone has confidence, they tend to seek out opportunities, eagerly chasing anything that could potentially help them create the life of their dreams. Alternatively, someone lacking confidence will wait for things to happen. This is a sign they are waiting to be rescued, meaning they require a savior figure to be free. Since an Alpha Male is his own savior figure, apathy has no place in the Alpha Male lifestyle.

- **Avoiding Eye Contact:** Anyone who avoids eye contact is either a liar or someone with a complete lack of self-confidence. Few things appear as submissive as being unable to maintain healthy eye contact with another person.

- **Constantly Apologizing:** It is one thing to apologize for stepping on a person's foot, or for making a mistake. It's quite something else to apologize for everything, even things that aren't your fault in any way, shape, or form. This is nothing short of an attempt to make everyone else happy at your own expense. Again, not something an Alpha Male would ever do.

Signs of True Confidence

Now that you have an idea of some of the common habits of insecure people, it's time to take a look at the signs of true confidence. These are the habits that any Alpha Male will practice every day, making them stand out from the rest of the crowd. Some signs of true confidence include:

- **Strong Body Language:** Such things as good posture, uncrossed arms, a wide stance, and a powerful stride reflect confidence. All of these are examples of strong body language, something that engenders respect and confidence in those around you. Being able to maintain eye contact with another person is another example.

- **Being well-groomed:** When you invest the time, effort, and money into taking care of your body, you tell the rest of the world that you are worth it. This not only makes you more attractive to those you interact with, but it also demonstrates the fact that you possess high levels of self-confidence.

- **Being well dressed:** In addition to taking the time and effort to care for your skin, hair, and overall physical self, it is vital that you put the same time and effort into the clothes you wear. Wearing average clothes will make you look average; when you dress in clothes that fit well, that are stylish, and that stand out, you send the message that you are confident and capable.

- **Being Supportive:** Whether it's lending an ear, a shoulder to cry on, or actual assistance for someone who's having a hard time, being supportive is a sign that you are a true Alpha Male. This is because Alphas know they have enough ability to not only ensure their own success but to help others achieve success as well. A truly confident man doesn't need to put others down to feel good about himself. Instead, he takes pride and satisfaction in raising others up.

- **Integrity:** Saying what you mean and keeping the promises you make are signs of true confidence. Alpha Males will not tell people only what they want to hear, nor will they make promises they can't keep. Furthermore, they will have a code of conduct that they keep regardless of circumstances. An Alpha Male will never compromise his values.

Steps to Building Confidence

While you may already have some of these positive habits in your life, others may need to be developed from scratch. Fortunately, the process of developing any habit is fairly easy and straight forward. The trick is to find a behavior that embodies the habit and to practice that behavior daily. Eventually, the behavior will become second nature, making it and its qualities a part of your everyday life.

The following are some behaviors to practice to develop the habit of confidence:

- **Improve your Appearance:** As mentioned earlier, appearance is a huge part of self-confidence. This goes for grooming as well as the clothes you wear. Therefore, the first step to developing confidence is to go through your closet and get rid of all the clothes that are old, worn, or ordinary. Replace them with clothes that make you look and feel your best.

Additionally, change your haircut. Stop going to the ten-dollar place and spend the cash for a proper stylist to give you the makeover you deserve. Give yourself thirty days to achieve these goals of improving your personal appearance.

- **Become Sociable:** Anyone who has struggled with insecurity will know how hard it can be to interact with strangers. However, the only way to build confidence is to face your fears. Therefore, the next step is to begin interacting with people regularly. Strike up conversations with baristas or cashiers, asking about their day. Maintain eye contact with them as you do, ensuring you connect with them in a meaningful way. Take thirty days to develop this skill, starting slowly but being strong in the end.

- **Take Charge of your Finances:** One of the main causes of low self-esteem is financial insecurity. While you may not be able to go out and double your income right away, you can take the time to ensure you eliminate bad spending habits. Take thirty days to go over your spending habits and eliminate all the unnecessary spending that results in you struggling financially. This will also provide the necessary cash for such things as better hairstyle and better clothes.

- **Take Charge of your Job:** Unless you are one of a very small minority, the chances are you are unhappy with your job in some way. Rather than accepting the situation, take the next thirty days to improve it. Either look for ways to improve the job you have or start looking for another job altogether. Freshen your resume and use your newly developed skills in socializing and looking your best to get a job that makes you happy as well as pays the bills.

- **Surround yourself with Friends:** One habit many people fall into is that of becoming isolated. This can significantly undermine a person's sense of self-esteem. Therefore, over the next thirty days, spend good quality time with those people who make you feel loved and appreciated. Invite them over for dinner or go out on the town. As long as you surround yourself with love and positivity, your confidence will continue to grow.

- **Find your Faith:** Every person needs a belief system that they can fall back on when times are hard, and to which they can aspire for self-betterment. This doesn't mean you have to choose a religion as such; rather, it means you should sit down and decide what your beliefs are. Furthermore, take the time to feel good about all the things you have. Be grateful for the people in your life, your opportunities, and even your desire to do better. In short, take the next thirty days to discover and write down the things that truly matter to you.

Impact of Confidence on Your Life

There is almost no end to the benefits that high levels of self-confidence can bring to your life. However, simply saying that may not be enough to keep you motivated when it comes to forming the habits needed to increase self-confidence. Instead, you might need a solid reward in sight, a prize to keep your eyes on to keep you moving in the right direction. The following are a few examples of the prizes that await someone with high self-confidence:

- **Increased Attractiveness:** Habits such as maintaining eye contact, dressing and grooming for success, and the like do more than just increase your sense of confidence. They serve to make you more attractive to others. Therefore, as you develop these habits, you will make yourself more desirable in the eyes of others. This includes women, potential employers, landlords, salespeople, and others who might hold sway over your future success. The confidence you exude when interacting with these people will often serve to put you closer to the life of your dreams.

- **Increased Opportunity:** One thing that confidence allows you to do is to step outside your comfort zone. This will enable you to find opportunities that might not have been available to you otherwise. The more opportunities you create, the more likely you are to achieve the success you both desire and deserve.

- **Better Choices:** When you struggle with insecurity, you tend to make decisions out of fear rather than out of desire. You might settle for a job that you know you can do instead of pursuing the job of your dreams. Likewise, you might settle for a woman that makes you "happy enough" instead of chasing the one that will make every day feel like Christmas. However, when you have high levels of confidence, you will make better choices, and those choices will help you to create the life of your dreams.

Chapter 9: Alpha Male Habit #2: Persistence

One of the biggest misconceptions regarding success is that it should somehow be instantaneous. In a world of immediate gratification, from fast food to next-day delivery, people have become accustomed to getting what they want without delay. If you take the time to observe the situation, you will notice a sinister truth; most things that can be achieved instantly aren't worth achieving. Take food, for example; any food that can be prepared in five minutes or less will not be the kind of food you write home about. On the other hand, a meal for which you had to wait half an hour or more was usually well worth the wait.

This is true in all areas of life, not just food. Any significant success will take time to achieve. Unfortunately, this is where most people fail. They don't have the single quality necessary to achieve the worthwhile results: persistence. Alpha Males, by contrast, possess the persistence needed to achieve those lofty goals, the ones that lead to life-changing success. This chapter will discuss some of the ways in which persistence pays off, as well as ways to develop the habit of being persistent.

Avoiding the Easy Path

Sometimes you will be faced with two choices at the most critical junctures in your life. The first choice is the easy choice, the one that requires the least amount of time, effort, and resources on your part. This is the choice that promises instant gratification. The other choice is the hard choice, the one that demands greater amounts of time, energy and resources to see the finished result. Although this choice proves more demanding in every way, it always promises to deliver results that are worth the extra investment. This is why the harder choice is often referred to as the "right choice" by Alpha Males.

When you make the harder choice, two things happen. First, you protect yourself from inferior results. When you turn away from the drive-in window at the fast-food restaurant, you protect yourself from the processed meats, fatty oils, and foods heavy in starch and salt that such places offer. In other words, you protect your body from excess weight, clogged arteries, and high blood pressure. No amount of time saved is worth that cost.

The second thing that happens when you make the harder choice is that you set yourself up for greater success. Sure, going to a good restaurant that serves freshly prepared food might cost more, and it will definitely take more time to get your food, but the finished product will be infinitely better than the poison you would be eating out of a paper bag. Your body and mind will be healthier and happier, improving your very quality of life. Eventually, as an Alpha Male, you will begin to see the harder choice as usually being the more attractive one.

How Persistence Turns the Tables

The idea of better results requiring greater effort can be seen in all areas of life. One such area is that of sculpting your body. Given a choice between going to the gym and staying home to watch TV, most people choose the easier option. The result is that the average person tends to be overweight, short of energy, and ultimately low on self-esteem. Those who choose to go to the gym wind up with higher levels of physical health, mental health, and general sense of wellbeing, which lead ultimately to greater self-esteem.

Furthermore, the person who goes to the gym has the option of going for perhaps twenty minutes a day three times a week, or for an hour a day five times a week. Again, the individual who makes the harder choice will gain the best results. In the end, the choice between easy and hard is always present. The more you choose the hard road, the better your outcome will inevitably be.

Another way that persistence can pay off is by wearing down resistance. Take, for example, the case of someone chasing after the job of their dreams. At first, they may not get the job, as it might go to someone with more experience, or as is so often the case, who knows someone on the inside. Most people would see that first shot as having been their one chance for success and walk away resigned to never getting that job. In contrast, an Alpha Male will persist in his efforts, sending in application after application, going on interview after interview. Eventually, the resistance will be broken, and the persistence will win the day. The Alpha Male realizes one simple secret, namely the fact that the result is what counts, not the time or effort it takes to achieve the result.

Stone is much harder than water, so rain will bounce off of a stone wall without leaving a trace. However, if stone is exposed to a constant water source, it will eventually wear away. The Grand Canyon, one of the world's largest valleys, was created by a river gradually eating away at the stone. This is one of nature's examples of how persistence can win out against all the odds.

What Persistence Says About A Man

Persistence is a quality that can easily be seen by others, and it says a lot about the man being observed. One thing persistence says about a man is that he is willing to do whatever it takes to achieve his goals. This means that he is not addicted to immediate gratification nor inclined to settle for lesser victories. Instead, he is dedicated to creating the very best results possible.

Another thing persistence says about a man is that he isn't lazy. Only a person who is full of energy and passion can remain persistent until their goal is achieved. These attributes are very attractive, not only to women but also to businessmen, bosses, and leaders of all types who are looking for the best men to bring onto their team. Thus, when an Alpha Male uses his persistence to achieve his goals, he draws attention to himself, the type of attention that will open all sorts of doors and put countless opportunities within his reach.

Finally, when a man is persistent, he demonstrates the fact that he knows what he wants. This means that his life is already on a trajectory toward success. Alpha Males have a strong sense of what they want, meaning that they are moving toward a destination.

Examples of Persistence in Our World

Ironically enough, some of the technology that has led to a culture accustomed to instant gratification owes its existence to technology that took unrelenting persistence to develop. Thomas Edison went through one thousand failed attempts before discovering the design that ultimately changed the world we live in today.

Henry Ford persisted through five bankruptcies before finally establishing the Ford Motor Company.

Walt Disney persisted through multiple failed businesses before reaching his breakthrough, a breakthrough that has changed the world of entertainment forever.

Albert Einstein persisted through many years of struggle before finally realizing the theories that would revolutionize the world of science.

Dr. Seuss, the world-renowned author of children's books, was rejected twenty-seven times before finally getting his first book published.

Michael Jordan was dropped from the basketball team at his high school for not meeting expectations.

Vincent van Gogh only sold one painting in his lifetime, yet his work is considered unparalleled in the art world today.

NASA experienced twenty failures in twenty-eight attempts to send a rocket into space.

These are but a few of the many examples of people who persisted through failure and struggled to achieve their goals. The lesson to be learned is that persistence is the key to success. It doesn't matter who you are or where you come from. You can have every resource at your disposal and still suffer countless setbacks before achieving success. You may be bankrupt and without prospects, yet success lies just around the corner, waiting for you to discover it. Only when you persist will you reach the final destination, the one where all the struggle and hardship pay off. Then you can enjoy the fruits of your success: the life of your dreams.

Chapter 10: Alpha Male Habit # 3: Frame

Another critical habit to form to develop an Alpha Male mindset is that of maintaining a dominant frame. In this case, a frame is an individual's outlook on reality. It is the framework from which they perceive the world around them. Every single person operates within their own unique frame, meaning that no two people see reality in exactly the same way. Different realities can collide from time to time, creating a competition of sorts. One reality must submit to the other for both people to coexist. As an Alpha Male, you rarely want to submit to someone else's frame. Instead, you must be the one to establish the reality in which everyone else exists. This chapter will discuss the impact that controlling the frame will have on your life, as well as numerous methods for developing the ability to create and maintain a dominant frame.

The Trap of Compromise

Many traditions teach the importance of compromise, asserting that when everyone is willing to give a little in a situation, no one has to lose. This theory sounds wonderful, but it is one of the countless theories that work far better on paper than in reality. The truth of the matter is that every situation contains a certain momentum. As one person gives in to the demands of the other, they begin to move in a negative direction; despite the other person reciprocating, they continue to move in a positive direction, taking as much as they can until they are ultimately the winner. This doesn't mean that one person is good and the other bad, it is just a reflection of human nature. In fact, it reflects the hard wiring of all species; any time animals interact, one will attain dominance while the others become submissive.

This is the trap of compromise. Every time you give in to another person's demands, it not only undermines your position, but it also strengthens the position of the other person. Therefore, even the smallest concession can turn into the first step down a very slippery slope, one that will see you at the bottom while the other person is at the top. Therefore, you must never give an inch when you have a clear idea of the goal you want to achieve. Only by holding fast to your vision will you have any chance of achieving that goal. This is one way that you control the frame.

Another trap of compromise is that every time you concede to accommodate someone else's goals or desires, you are letting them live your life. Now, rather than your time and effort leading to achieving your goals, they lead to achieving the goals of someone else. Eventually, it is as though your life is no longer yours. It's as if the other person has two lives now, or even more depending on how many people are submitting to their will. This may not happen overnight; it usually evolves over a long period. Giving an inch here and an hour there may seem small at the moment, but over time those small sacrifices add up, resulting in you sacrificing miles and years in the end. The best way to avoid this pitfall is to never compromise for anyone, ever.

Establishing Your Personal Frame

The common understanding of compromise is that the opposite of compromise is tyranny. In other words, if you are unwilling to give a little, it must mean that you intend to control everyone else. This isn't the true opposite of compromise at all. Instead, the true opposite is *independence.* When you are unwilling to sacrifice your ideals or goals for someone else's happiness, you are independent of what other people feel, do, or say. This is the face of true freedom. Therefore, to be free of the influences and controls of others, you must avoid compromise. The best way to achieve this goal is to establish your personal frame.

One of the main elements of your personal frame is your set of goals. When you have specific goals that you want to achieve, then that becomes the frame of your reality. Any action, idea, thought, or word that leads to the achievement of your goals fits into your frame. Everything else falls outside your frame, as it will likely only impede your progress, or worse, lead you away from your desired destination. Peer pressure, for example, won't affect you when you have a solid frame. While others may submit to the pressure and change their actions, you will stay the course, holding true to the values that will lead you to success.

In the end, as well as being your perception of life as a whole, your frame is your perception of your personal life. It is how you see yourself in the here and now, as well as the vision of where you see yourself in the future. It is about your actions, your beliefs, and your vision of what success truly means. In this light, creating a strong frame isn't about controlling others; instead, it is about gaining ultimate control over your own life and never allowing outside influences to take that control away.

Maintaining Your Personal Frame

Once you have established your frame, the next step is to maintain that frame at all costs. As just noted, to maintain the integrity of your frame you must avoid the trap of compromise at all costs. Another bad habit that needs to be broken to maintain your personal frame is that of being reactionary. All too often, it can seem necessary to try to convince others that your vision, values, or goals are right. However, every time you try to convince another person of your frame you are actually submitting to theirs; when you maintain your frame, you aren't worried about what others think or say. In fact, you are willing to lose support from those who don't see things your way.

It's a bit like driving a bus; as the driver, you decide the direction the bus is going. If some of the passengers don't like it, they can get off at the next stop. Those who choose to stay on are the people who agree with your direction and thus are the ones you want by your side.

This leads to a very important rule that every Alpha Male applies to their life. That rule is to gain control over your emotions. Any time a person lashes out in anger or frustration, they abandon their own frame and become consumed by the frame of another. Such outbursts only serve to reveal insecurity within the individual; insecurity born of doubt, low self-esteem, and all the other elements that are contrary to an Alpha Male's mindset. As an Alpha Male, you must maintain emotional equilibrium at all times. Always stay focused on your goals and your frame. If someone else disagrees with or challenges your frame, realize that you don't have anything to prove. By staying true to yourself, you will gain the respect of those who are truly worthwhile. Anyone who doesn't respect your Alpha Male qualities is someone you are better off without.

For example, let's say you wanted to sell your house, and you were asking two hundred thousand dollars for it. Numerous people may come along and make counteroffers, usually for far less than the asking price. By avoiding compromise, you ensure that you achieve your success, not the success of someone else. Furthermore, you never have to get angry or frustrated with any person who makes a counteroffer. All you have to do is reject each counteroffer with dignity and respect. The fact that they don't want to spend the money you are asking for doesn't mean you are in the wrong. You aren't trying to sell your house to any particular person anyway. The truth of the matter is that it doesn't matter who buys your house. The important thing is that you sell your house and that you get the price you are asking. Eventually, a buyer will come along and agree on terms. Then *you* are the winner as you held fast to your frame, maintaining your integrity and vision every step of the way. Ironically enough, the person who will buy the house will usually be one of the people who made counteroffer after counteroffer trying to get you to compromise, thus proving that your frame was reasonable after all.

Chapter 11: Alpha Male Habit # 4: Physical Appearance

One thing that cannot be overstated is the simple fact that being an Alpha Male is about so much more than having a perfectly sculpted physique. Confidence, charm, purpose, and other similar qualities are all vital elements of the Alpha Male personality. However, none of this means that exercise and bodybuilding should be ignored or avoided. Just because they are not the be-all and end-all to being an Alpha Male, they still play a pivotal role. Therefore, one habit that is recommended for developing your Alpha Male lifestyle is to work on your physique daily. This chapter will highlight some of the more common and effective methods for creating a physical appearance that will attract the right attention from the right people.

Creating A Healthy Appearance

When it comes to creating the physical appearance of an Alpha Male, you must begin by focusing on your health. No amount of muscle tone will show through unwanted pounds around the waist or on your arms. Therefore, before going to the gym to lift weights and build those biceps, you need to achieve the ideal weight for your height and age. Since this varies from person to person, it is recommended that you either do some research online to determine your ideal weight or partner with a trainer who can guide you in the right direction.

Diet is the most important element when it comes to controlling your weight. Regardless of whether you are looking to add pounds to a skinny frame or take off pounds from a rounder frame, the foods you eat, along with the portions and times of day you eat your meals, will significantly affect your progress. Therefore, even before you begin any exercise regimen, you must get rid of all the junk foods and start eating healthy foods such as vegetables, fruits, and high-protein foods like eggs, beans, and fish. The latter are excellent sources of protein and other nutrients that can help create a healthy body weight no matter which direction you need to go. Also, drinking plenty of fluids, mostly water or milk, will help to give you the body mass needed to make all other efforts worthwhile.

Along with eating the right foods, it is recommended that you begin a regimen of daily supplements to assist you in changing your body mass. Any nutrition store or reputable gym will have plenty of vitamins, nutritional supplements, and other items that will help to burn fat, increase weight, or help you in whatever way you require. While many people shy away from supplements, they can actually make a huge difference in how soon you begin to see results. Taking fat-busting pills on their own won't get the job done. However, when combined with a healthy diet and exercise the results will be exponentially better. The trick is to not rely on any single solution; instead, implement several different efforts at the same time. This increases not only your chances of success but the very level of success you can achieve.

The third prong of your attack will take the shape of cardio workouts. Whether you are trying to lose weight or improve your body's tone, cardio workouts are essential for your progress. Combined with diet and supplements, these workouts will impact every single area of your health and wellbeing.

Integrating multiple approaches is one of two key ingredients when it comes to creating a healthy physical appearance; the second ingredient is consistency. Unless you create *the habits* of exercising, eating right, and taking nutritional supplements, you will only achieve nominal results. Even worse, those results may not last if you allow yourself to go back to the old habits that robbed you of your physical health and wellbeing in the first place. Therefore, to ensure the best and most long-lasting results, you must remain consistent in your efforts. You should eat healthily and take supplements every single day. When it comes to exercise, you should practice five days a week, giving your body two full days to rest and recover. You can choose to skip exercise when you go on vacation if the opportunity doesn't present itself; however, you must return to your regimen as soon as you get home.

Improving Your Shoulders and Arms

Once you get your overall physical appearance where it needs to be, you can start working on the more detailed aspects of creating an Alpha Male appearance. One of the main areas of focus needs to be on your shoulders and arms. After all, the broader your shoulders are, the more respect you will command just by walking into a room. This is one reason why men in uniform often appear larger than life. While the uniform itself adds a lot to their appearance, it is their broad shoulders filling out the uniform that actually attracts attention. Additionally, having strong, healthy arms will go a long way to making an impact wherever you are, especially when you wear a t-shirt or short sleeves showing off your advanced muscle tone.

Fortunately, several easy exercises will help you create Alpha Male shoulders and arms in no time. Again, your results will only be equal to your efforts; therefore, you must spend time every week working on your arms and shoulders by performing the right exercises. Overhead presses are an excellent exercise for building broad shoulders. It is important to perform them correctly, using your arms and shoulders to lift the barbell and not your legs. Your legs should be straight at all times, thereby putting the focus of effort on your shoulders. Five sets of five repetitions each are all you need to do to start building the shoulders of your dreams.

Upright rows are another good exercise for building broad, strong shoulders. This is similar to an overhead press, but instead of pushing the barbell up over your head from shoulder height, you pull it up to your chin from your waist. You can choose to use a single dumbbell in each hand for both exercises if you need time to build your strength. Additionally, using dumbbells is safer if you have to exercise alone; any time you use barbells, especially with heavy weights, it is recommended that you work out with at least one partner who can spot you and help you to avoid injury.

Lateral raises and farmer's carries are two other exercises recommended for building strong shoulders. In the case of lateral raises, you will raise dumbbells from your waist to shoulder height, keeping your arms straight. As the name suggests, these raises are done with your arms pointing out at your sides. The farmer's carry is when you carry dumbbells at waist height, keeping your arms straight as you walk naturally. This puts the focus of the effort on your shoulders.

Exercises for building muscle tone in your arms are fairly common and well-known. Any bench press will help to increase muscle tone in your arms, as will any barbell curl exercise. Four of the best exercises to get you started are the close grip bench press, the standard barbell curl, triceps dips, and the hammer curl. These exercises will not only get your biceps well-formed; they will ensure that all muscles in your arms, shoulders and upper chest also get well-formed. Again, since these exercises require the use of a barbell, always work out with someone who will be able to assist you if something goes wrong.

Improving Your Waist and Legs

The last area you want to focus on is your upper body; you don't want to develop it first, leaving your waist and legs to look flimsy and weak. Therefore, you must implement exercises for your waist and legs before working on upper body, thereby giving your appearance a natural symmetry that will add to your visual appeal.

When it comes to shaping your waist, the most important thing to focus on is your diet. This is because your waistline is the first place where fat usually gets deposited. Only when you eat right will you have any chance of creating a waist that is appealing to others, and that gives you the confidence of an Alpha Male.

Several exercises can help you to trim your waistline down and keep it looking mean and lean for years to come. Ab wheel rollouts are one such exercise. An ab wheel is a piece of exercise equipment available at any gym. To do a rollout, you need to be on your knees, keeping your back straight or only slightly arched while slowly extending your upper body forward using the wheel. Hanging leg raises are another excellent exercise for trimming your waistline. Simply hang from a bar, much like you would if you were about to do chin-ups, but instead of lifting with your arms, bring your knees up to your chest. Although this sounds simple, it will work out your chest muscles, arm muscles, and shoulders in a very serious way.

Finally, there is the exercise known as the windshield wiper leg raise. This is where you lay on your back and lift your legs straight into the air, keeping them together and your knees straight. Then you move your legs from side to side while keeping your upper body in place. The motion looks a bit like windshield wipers going back and forth, hence the name.

Everyone's body is unique in a great many ways. One such way is that you will have certain muscle groups that are naturally stronger and better defined than others. For example, you might already have broad shoulders, or thick, muscular legs. Or, you might have strong arms or a slim stomach. The important thing is to invest your time and energy wisely. Therefore, spend less time developing the areas of your body already in decent shape. Instead, focus most of your time and effort on building your weaker areas. This will help to give you a more symmetrical look. You can choose to spend one day on all the exercises that focus on your strong points while taking individual days for each of the other areas that need more work.

Chapter 12: Alpha Male Habit # 5: Mental Toughness

While physical appearance can be all-important for making that first impression, it takes more than muscles to keep people, especially women, impressed for long. This is why Alpha Males possess an abundance of what is commonly referred to as mental toughness. Just as a strong body can remove many physical obstacles and withstand physical attacks, so too, a strong mind can overcome mental and emotional obstacles and withstand all sorts of negative assaults, both from without as well as from within. Mental toughness is the condition of having the strongest mind available, the kind of mind that can rise above any situation and prevail against all the odds. To achieve this mental toughness, you have to develop the habit of standing strong in your beliefs and pursuits. This chapter will discuss some of the key ways to achieve this goal, as well as the numerous advantages mental toughness will provide in all areas of your life.

Redefining Failure

Failure is something that every person experiences numerous times throughout their life. Unfortunately, it is also one of the most misunderstood situations that people face. Most see failure as the end of the road, where dreams and ambitions come crashing down in a fiery mess. They see failure as a painful experience that should be avoided at all costs. The result is that most people never step out of their comfort zone. This means that they choose a life of mediocrity rather than one where they turn their dreams into reality.

In contrast, Alpha Males are not only unafraid of leaving their comfort zone, they usually spend most of their existence there. This is because rather than fearing failure, Alphas embrace it. This might seem hard to understand at first, especially given the role that success plays in the life of an Alpha Male. However, it's how an Alpha embraces failure that makes all the difference. In the mind of an Alpha Male, failure isn't a painful experience, nor does it spell the end of a dream. Instead, it is a learning experience, one in which the Alpha Male can grow stronger, wiser, and ultimately better. They redefine failure, turning it into something positive rather than a negative.

To develop the Alpha Male trait of mental toughness, you must redefine failure. The first way to do this is to stop seeing failure as the end of the journey. Imagine you are driving somewhere you have never been before. If you take a wrong turn and begin to get lost, you don't simply give up and go home. Instead, you turn around, go back to where you made the wrong turn, and choose a different direction. This is precisely how failure can be seen. It is a wrong turn of sorts. Instead of giving up on a dream simply because the path you chose didn't work out, simply go back to square one and choose a different path. It isn't about which route you take to get to your destination; it's about arriving at the destination. Never, ever let failure cause you to quit. That is one of the most important habits to form when it comes to mental toughness.

Another way to redefine failure is to see it as a learning experience. Every time you fail to achieve a goal, rather than taking it personally, see it as a chance to learn and improve. Again, it took Thomas Edison one thousand attempts before he successfully created the electric light bulb. Each time, rather than getting frustrated or embarrassed, he became curious. He took the time to learn what each failure had to teach. It wasn't enough to know that a certain prototype didn't work; he wanted to know why. This is what ultimately led him to create the one that brought him success.

You can do the same thing in your life. Each time you fail, take a step back and replay the video in your mind. Why did you fail? What did you do wrong? Once you figure that out, you can try again, making sure you don't make the same mistakes. If you get shot down when asking a woman out on a date, ask yourself where it went wrong. It won't take long to figure out when you lost control of the situation or when she lost interest. Figure out the words or the actions that failed and remove them from your next attempt. The same can be applied to job interviews that went wrong, public speeches that don't achieve your intended goal, or any other situation where failure occurs. Rather than giving up or losing confidence, take the opportunity to grow with every failure you encounter. Eventually, you will almost be happy when you fail because you will see it as an opportunity for personal growth.

Establishing Discipline

Another element of mental toughness is discipline. Imagine a person who has an entire gym at their disposal, with all the equipment, and even a staff of personal trainers on hand twenty-four hours a day, seven days a week. All of those resources are for nothing if the individual doesn't put in the effort to exercise on a regular basis. The element needed to turn resources into results is discipline.

One form of discipline that forms mental toughness is staying focused on the task at hand. All too often, people get distracted by any number of things, like their cell phone, social media, or even their own imagination. They allow their minds to wander, causing their productivity to dip and the quality of their results to suffer. In contrast, an Alpha Male exercises great mental discipline, staying singularly focused on whatever task he is performing no matter how large or small, no matter how important or insignificant. That is one of the things that set the Alpha Male apart from everyone else. He will put one hundred percent of his attention and effort into every single thing he does. This ensures he has greater productivity and that he produces the best results every time. Eliminate all distractions whenever you address a task, and invest all of your effort into anything you do.

Another type of discipline that Alpha Males possess is that of emotional discipline. This is what an Alpha uses to avoid reacting to something in an emotionally charged way. It can be all too easy to snap at someone who says the wrong thing, especially when you are stressed out because things aren't going according to plan. What sets Alpha Males apart is that rather than letting their emotions get the best of them, they always keep their emotions in check. One way is to stop letting things affect you personally. Don't let what other people say or do change your mood; don't allow others to impact your emotional wellbeing. Let them say or do what they want. The trick is to stay focused on your opinions, your vision, and most importantly, your beliefs. Just because they don't agree with you doesn't mean you aren't right. Additionally, it's not your job to get them to see things your way. Live your life according to *your* vision and *your* rules, and let the rest of the world do *their* thing.

Finally, there is the aspect of discipline regarding how you manage your time. In a world filled with all sorts of distractions and responsibilities, it can be all too easy to get swept up in the momentum of life. When this happens, it causes a person to lose their sense of direction and perspective. Sometimes they aren't sure where they are going, and they never seem to have enough time to get there. Alpha Males will always seem to be in charge of their life, rather than a hapless victim of it. This is because they create a schedule that keeps them from getting swept away by the fast pace of modern-day life. When you create a daily routine, including when you go to bed, when you wake up, and when you perform your functions throughout the day, you create a sense of order that eliminates the stress and chaos that affect countless people every day. This discipline of time management enables you to spend quality time doing the things that matter most, such as spending time with loved ones and family, focusing on personal development, and chasing your dreams and ambitions. It's not about finding the right time to do things; it's about using your time in the right way to get everything done.

Staying Positive

The final habit to form when it comes to developing mental toughness is that of staying positive. Even the strongest, smartest, and most capable of Alpha Males will have bad days. Things don't always go according to plan, people can be negative and toxic, and situations can arise that test even the strongest of resolves. These things are unavoidable; however, this doesn't mean that those bad times have to change who you are. This is one of the most important lessons in the life of an Alpha Male: never let events define you, always be the author of who you are.

One way to always control your identity is to stay positive no matter what. A good way to do this is to remember that no matter how bad times get, they are temporary. It's a bit like the weather. Even the fiercest storm will end eventually, giving way to sunny, peaceful days once again. Alpha Males know this, and that is how they manage to stay calm and positive no matter how bad things get. They know that you can't control bad times any more than you can control the weather, so they don't lose energy trying to do so. They also know that it gets darkest before dawn, so even the worst of times will give way to better times once again.

Another reason Alpha Males stay positive is that they don't fear the worst times. Sure, bad times can have devastating effects on anyone's life. However, Alpha Males know that they can rebuild their lives no matter how much devastation they face. Furthermore, they take such opportunities to rebuild their lives better than they were before. It's a bit like if a house gets destroyed by a tornado. Rather than getting all emotional and bitter about it, an Alpha Male will see it as a chance to build an even better house. This is similar to redefining failure. When you see even the darkest, most tragic events as a chance for self-improvement, you will maintain a positive mindset as you look to the future and see how much better things will be as a result of those darker times. Therefore, rather than focusing on the negative aspect of an event, learn to focus on the positive results such events can lead to. This will keep your mood positive and buoyant no matter what situation you find yourself in, thus enabling you to see things clearly and remain in control of your actions while others flounder around you.

Chapter 13: Alpha Male Habit # 6: Charm

A common trait often associated with being an Alpha Male is that of arrogance. This association is completely mistaken, and it paints Alpha Male's in a negative light. Arrogantly bragging about your abilities and achievements (usually while belittling others in the process) demonstrates insecurity and jealousy, traits that are not consistent with the Alpha Male mindset. True Alpha Males demonstrate another trait when interacting with others, one that reveals their unrivaled strength of character. This is the trait of charm. Whether it is in appearance, approach, or how they speak, Alpha Males will exude charm in every way imaginable. Therefore, to further your Alpha Male development, you must master the art of charm. This habit will ensure others see you as a confident, capable Alpha Male standing head and shoulders above the rest.

Instilling Charm in Your Appearance

As already mentioned in this book, your appearance is almost always the first element of your personality others discover. Therefore, if you allow your appearance to be sloppy and unimpressive, you put yourself in a negative position when interacting with others. Since their first impression of you will be unfavorable, you will have to rely on your other qualities to dig yourself out of the hole you put yourself in. This is why it is vital to ensure that your appearance gets your interactions off to the right start, one where you are respected and admired even before you have opened your mouth.

Fortunately, it takes little effort to instill charm into your appearance. The first thing you want to do is get rid of any clothes that are dingy, worn, oversized, or just sloppy in appearance. Being casual doesn't mean you have to look homeless. Instead of opting for worn-out sneakers, invest in some comfortable, well-made shoes that combine aesthetics with comfort and function. You should always look at ease wherever you are, whatever you are doing; the right shoes will help you achieve that look while also telling others that you have an eye for style and fashion.

The same goes for all of your clothing. Don't settle for a floppy sweatshirt that advertises the store from which it was purchased. That won't set you apart from the crowd in any way. Instead, invest in shirts that stand out, whether it's the color, the cut, or the overall style. Always go for something as stylish as it is unique. Clothes don't have to just be about hiding your nakedness; they should be about expressing yourself. Treat them as the medium for your artistic flair. Choose shirts that flatter your shape and skin tone, and that show off your arms as you begin to develop your Alpha Male physique.

Pants should be seen in the same way. Rather than wearing baggy jeans that are as common as a ten-dollar haircut, opt for pants that provide a little more flair. You don't have to wear a suit and tie all the time, but a good pair of fashionable pants can make all the difference when it comes to being noticed for all the right reasons. You want your pants to accentuate your body's shape, so choose the colors and styles needed to make you look like the proverbial million dollars. This will mean you need to take the time to try on different options to ensure you get the most for your money. Don't expect the pair of pants on the skinny dude in the poster to work, necessarily. Instead, always recognize your body's shape and work with it accordingly. No matter what size or shape you are now, some clothes can give you the Alpha Male appearance that will turn heads wherever you go.

Instilling Charm in Your Approach

In addition to affecting how you look, charm can make all the difference when it comes to your approach. This is true in every area, including approaching a woman, a potential boss, a potential client, or any other person. Being an Alpha Male affects every aspect of your life. It's not as though you turn it on when it matters and turn it off when it doesn't. One of the secrets that make Alpha Males so successful is that they are the same twenty-four hours a day, seven days a week. So, your approach needs to be one of charm and poise no matter whether you are trying to attract a woman or pay the guy who mows your lawn.

Before forming any new habits in this area, the first thing you need to do is ensure you don't have any bad habits. Being too needy is one such bad habit that needs to be eliminated right away. Never appear desperate when it comes to achieving your goal, no matter how important that goal is. Neediness and desperation are signs of weakness. Instead, exercise patience. Always approach a person or situation with calm confidence, the sort of attitude that tells them that while you are confident of success, you won't be intimidated if things don't turn out the way you expect.

How you walk is one way to demonstrate this attitude. Never appear as though you are rushing around like a madman, running from one obligation to another. Instead, develop a walk that is both purposeful and relaxed. Long, natural strides will give an air of authority, while a slow but steady pace will give you an air of relaxed confidence. Neither hurried nor sluggish, this walk will set you apart from the rest who are usually running around like the proverbial chickens with their heads cut off.

How you carry yourself is equally important when it comes to mastering the art of charm. No one takes the "macho man" image seriously, so walking around like a gym junky on steroids won't get the attention you desire. Instead, you should maintain an upright posture while keeping your body fairly relaxed. Your arms should hang loosely down by your side when standing and should swing freely but not excessively when walking. A good rule of thumb is always to feel balanced. When you are walking, you should feel as though you could stop suddenly without falling either forward or backward. Alternatively, when you are standing, you should feel relaxed yet firm, as though someone could push you unexpectedly and not knock you over. Keeping your feet apart is a good way to achieve this balance. Also, always keep your shoulders square and your chin up as this will give you an added air of command.

Instilling Charm in How You Speak

The final area where you need to master the art of charm is in how you speak. Just as the pace with which you walk says everything about you, so too, the pace with which you speak will tell others who you really are. How you say your words can prove just as important as the words themselves. When you speak too quickly, it demonstrates anxiety; speaking too slow can suggest that you are disinterested, or worse, a bit stupid. To demonstrate confidence, intelligence, and ultimately charm, you need to learn to speak in a calm yet purposeful pace, one in which your words are enunciated and deliberate. Your speech should feel as balanced as your stride.

What you say can make or break you in the eyes, or ears, of others. Many men fall into the trap of trying to use fancy words to impress others. They either wind up using words incorrectly or even worse, they use big, fancy words correctly but only confuse those they are speaking to. Therefore, focus on the content rather than the words themselves. Only use words you fully understand and are comfortable with. The important thing is to express yourself clearly and thoroughly. Anything else is just wasted and makes it appear as though you are trying to impress someone.

Another element of charm within speech is that of offering compliments. Whether you are telling a woman that she is beautiful or telling the lawn guy that he did a tremendous job, paying someone a sincere, heartfelt compliment will always come across as charming. However, the key is that a compliment has to be sincere. Rather than just saying something shallow and mundane such as "You look beautiful today," you will want to focus on a particular quality, such as "That color really brings out the color of your eyes," or "Those shoes really look adorable on you." When you take the time to add details to your compliment, they tell the other person that you are sincere in your words, and that makes all the difference between a compliment and a pick-up line or shallow attempt at ingratiation.

Perhaps the most important aspect of charm when it comes to speaking is that of knowing when not to speak. Anyone who tries to dominate the conversation will be seen as overbearing or bullying, qualities that don't attract positive reactions. In contrast, when a man sits silently, his eyes fixed on the person speaking, it gives an air of respect, interest, and true connection. Sometimes the best way into a woman's heart isn't the words you say, or even how you say them, but it is the ability to stay silent while listening intently to what *she* has to say. Good eye contact, relaxed nods, and a genuine smile or frown at the appropriate time will convey that you are sincerely listening to her, not zoning out wondering who will win tonight's game or whether she has a prettier sister. This is how you can remain active in a conversation without having to say a single word.

Chapter 14: Alpha Male Habit # 7: Purpose

Another vital habit practiced by all Alpha Males is that of living by core values and staying true to purpose. All of the charm, confidence, and skill in the world won't amount to much if you don't have good reason to put them to use. This is where purpose comes into play. In essence, purpose is the direction you travel in when living your life. Without purpose, you simply drift along, letting the current take you where it will. However, when you have a purpose, it's like having a compass that you can use to ensure your actions and circumstances are taking you where you want to go. Purpose can also embody your core values. By taking the time to discover and develop your personal values, you ensure that your actions and efforts will always be consistent, providing stability and reliability in your life. Not only will that help you to achieve your goals, but it will also make you stand out in the eyes of others. The more reliable and constant you are, the more others will trust and respect you.

Discovering Your Core Values

The first step toward developing purpose in your life is to take the time to discover your core values. Most people are so fixated on achieving success or impressing others that they will do anything necessary to realize those goals. This leaves them feeling empty and uncertain when it comes to their own beliefs and desires. In contrast, an Alpha Male has a clear set of core values that tells him who he is, what he wants, and what he is willing to do to accomplish his goals. Such a values system not only sets the Alpha Male up for success, but it also gives him strength, hope, and courage in times of failure and distress.

Discovering your core values requires a fair bit of soul searching. Therefore, take as much time and effort as is needed to conscientiously accomplish this task. An important element of this task is to write everything down. Rather than grabbing the nearest scrap of paper or partially used napkin, give this the respect it deserves and buy a proper journal. Devote this journal to your personal development as an Alpha Male and as a person in general. Although some may see keeping a journal as effeminate or nerdy, the truth of the matter is that the strongest, most successful people keep journals almost religiously.

Once you have your journal and pen, set aside some time to sit and contemplate. Make sure you will be undisturbed and turn off all distractions, including your phone, the TV, and even the radio. Next, write down the question, "What am I passionate about?" If those words don't kick your mind into action, you can create a different question, such as "What makes me truly happy?" or "What do I want most in life?" or "If I had ten million dollars what would I do?" In short, you are trying to find the things that give you meaning, true happiness, and that make your life worthwhile. When you have the question that works for you, take the time to listen to what pops into your mind. Write everything down, no matter how ridiculous it may seem. This isn't a test, nor is it something that anyone else ever has to see. Therefore, be honest and don't hold back. Write down everything that comes into your mind.

Next, reduce your list to about five items. Chances are that any more than five are the result of external influences, a passing interest, or redundant interests. All in all, you should only have up to five or six things that truly inspire you, things you would pursue if money were no object. If you have trouble with reducing your list, then try to prioritize it in order of importance. If you still can't get your list down to five simply break the list in half, taking the top five for values to focus on now and the others as values to address later on down the road.

The values you list shouldn't be goals as such; rather, they should be the values that underlie your goals. Therefore, marrying a particular person or finding a specific job aren't values. Having a happy home life or a satisfying career, however, are. The following is a short list of values that will help get you started:

- ✔ Discipline
- ✔ Freedom
- ✔ Happiness
- ✔ Spirituality
- ✔ Fun
- ✔ Physical health and wellbeing
- ✔ Knowledge
- ✔ Power
- ✔ Financial stability
- ✔ Success
- ✔ Family
- ✔ Self-expression
- ✔ Integrity

Defining Yourself by Your Values

Once you have listed your values, the next step is to separate your list into two categories. One category will be those values such as integrity, discipline, knowledge, and the like that define you as a person. The other category will be such values as financial stability, physical health and wellbeing, freedom and the like that define the life you want to live. When you have divided your list, you are ready to begin defining yourself based on your values.

Next, write down your personal values on a fresh page. Now, try to imagine a role model that personifies those qualities. There might be someone in your personal life that possesses them in abundance, or you might choose a character in literature, the movies or religious texts. Again, since this isn't a test, there is no wrong answer. Instead, this is about you finding your ideal. It doesn't matter who personifies that idea. All that matters is that you have that ideal clear in your mind so that you can measure your words and actions accordingly. If your ideal is Superman, then you have Superman in your mind. Any time you find yourself in a challenging situation you simply ask yourself, "What would Superman do?" This will bring your values to mind, ensuring that your actions are consistent with integrity, discipline, and knowledge.

It's not about becoming Superman, rather it's about becoming your ideal self. Eventually, you won't need an icon to embody your values. Instead, you will embody them so thoroughly that you only need to ask yourself what *you* would do, and those values will be right there. Alternatively, you might not even have to ask the question at all. Your values will be so ingrained in your character that you will only have to act naturally to do the right thing. The best part is that as you become your ideal self, others will look to you for inspiration, using your example to become their best self.

Still, this isn't about impressing others or becoming the hero. Instead, this is about establishing your values for your own peace of mind. So much stress and anxiety revolve around guilt and uncertainty, things that come when values are either ignored or simply unknown. When you take the time to discover and implement your values, you create a life that is honest and true, one that provides peace of mind and a clear conscience. This is at the very heart of being an Alpha Male. When you live by your values, you have the strength of character that keeps you safe, and that makes you stand out from those who flounder around aimlessly as they struggle to find their way.

Establishing Your Purpose

The other half of your list will be those values that best define your life, such as financial stability, physical health and wellbeing, and freedom. Although these values affect who you are as a person, they tend to describe your lifestyle rather than your core beliefs. Physical health and wellbeing require you to exercise and eat right, things that are part of your lifestyle, unlike integrity, which stems from a state of mind. These are the values that establish your purpose. Write these values in your journal on a separate page and envision the lifestyle that personifies them. You can use the lifestyle of someone you know, a famous person, or something that is of your own creation. All that matters is that you create an image of the reality you wish to achieve. This will give you a destination to pursue, and this destination will become your purpose.

When your life has a purpose, it has direction. This helps you to make better and easier decisions throughout life. For example, deciding what job to pursue becomes far easier when you have a sense of direction. If a job takes you closer to financial stability and freedom, then it is a good fit for you. Alternatively, if it fails to provide those elements, then it is a bad fit as it takes you further away from the life you want to create.

This sense of purpose helps you to be in constant control of your life. By knowing what your dreams are, and thus what it will take to make those dreams come true, you know immediately whether something is good or bad just by its very nature. Furthermore, your personal values will help you to stay true to your principles as you plot a course that takes you to your ultimate destination, the life of your dreams. Every choice and decision you make will be purpose-driven, and this will give you the confidence and certainty that most people lack, making you the true Alpha Male in the group.

Chapter 15: Alpha Male Habit # 8: Self-Care

Numerous studies have shown a direct and significant link between self-care and self-esteem. When a person puts time and effort into their appearance and overall wellbeing every day, their self-esteem is strong and healthy. When people ignore their appearance and spend little to no time taking care of their personal needs, their self-esteem plummets. In fact, one sure way to help a person overcome depression is to force them to spend time grooming daily. Sadly, a study done in 2017 by AXE revealed that most men between the ages of 18 to 30 feel pressured by the "macho" image to ignore grooming and other forms of self-care since such things are considered effeminate. Common stereotypes suggest that tough men don't care about their image, causing many to equate grubbiness with masculinity. Alpha Males, by contrast, recognize the importance of self-care in all its forms. Therefore, a necessary habit to form when developing the Alpha Male lifestyle is to take care of yourself, both internally and externally. This chapter will reveal ways to achieve this goal, helping you to create a daily regimen that will cultivate your Alpha Male mindset.

Physical Self-Care

The first element of self-care that you need to establish is that of physical self-care. This covers a wide array of responsibilities, but they are all equally vital in terms of creating an Alpha Male lifestyle. As already discussed, the first step is to watch what you eat, with regard to both what types of food and how much food. Also, note that eating late at night has been proven to increase body fat and even adversely affect your sleep patterns, leaving you sluggish and tired the next day. Always make sure that you eat a healthy meal at least three hours before you plan on going to bed; this will ensure your body digests your food before shutting down to get the rest it needs.

Another element of physical self-care that is often overlooked is bathing. It is vital to shower each and every day, not just to avoid unpleasant odors but also to keep your body healthy and germ-free. The longer you go between showers, the less likely your body will be able to fight common sicknesses such as the cold or flu. Additionally, your skin can begin to suffer numerous consequences when you skip bathing, such as an increase in acne, clogged pores, and even rapid aging due to dehydration. This leads to another important issue, namely using hydrating soaps and lotions when you bathe. Avoid anything that claims to be shampoo and body wash all in one. Such items will only dry your scalp and skin, leaving you worse off after a shower than before. Use soaps and shampoos that restore moisture to skin and hair, as these will improve your physical appearance significantly.

Finally, there is the practice of pampering your body. Get massages regularly. Go to saunas or hot tubs to relax your muscles and soothe your mind. Although these practices seem indulgent, they are, in fact, essential for a healthy body and mind. Massages can do wonders when it comes to maintaining healthy muscles, blood flow, and oxygen flow throughout your body. Additionally, they help you to unwind in a way that makes stress and anxiety virtually evaporate from your body and mind. Since Alpha Males aren't worried about public perception when it comes to masculinity, they will get massages and even take bubble baths to ensure a happier and healthier state of physical wellbeing.

Mental Self-Care

Just as the body requires exercise to become healthy and strong, the mind requires its own type of exercise to thrive. Unfortunately, this is another area that many men ignore due to misguided stereotypes that imply "manly men" are never supposed to be seen with a book in their hands or wandering the galleries of a museum. Such "manly men", although physically strong, will remain mentally weak. Alpha Males know that to truly impress a woman, you need to have brains as well as brawn; therefore, they spend as much time and effort exercising their mind as they do their body.

Reading is one of the best mental exercises you can do. Reading ten to fifteen minutes per day is all it takes to boost your mental health, and is something that you can do any time of day and in any place, provided there is enough light and you can tune out the surrounding noise and distractions. Perhaps the best part of reading is that it provides countless conversations regarding the genres you like, the topics you read, and how those things affect your life. This will keep you interesting far after the "manly men" have lost their luster in a woman's eyes.

Learning new things can also go a long way to creating and maintaining mental health and wellbeing. Not only has learning been proven to improve memory and problem-solving skills, but it has also been shown to stave off such things as Alzheimer's and other disorders that affect people late in life. One of the most effective tools in this area is learning another language. Few things are as attractive as a man who can speak more than one language, so this is a win/win situation, to say the least. In addition to improving your mental acuity by learning another language, you will also really impress your lady by ordering dinner in the native language of the restaurant you take her to on date night. Not only will your woman admire you for your intellect, but the women around will also take note (usually to the detriment of their significant other).

Learning a new language requires only ten to fifteen minutes a day and can be done online at no cost. Trips to museums or other intellectually charged environments can be made once every couple of weeks or so, giving you a more intensive dose of mental exercise that helps develop the mind of a true Alpha Male.

Emotional Self-Care

Emotional self-care is something that can make all the difference when it comes to your overall state of mind. The more stressed and frustrated you are, the less confident and self-assured you will be. Therefore, you must spend time every day taking care of your emotional needs, much the way you do when it comes to taking care of your physical needs.

Effective emotional care is a two-sided coin. On the one side, the most important thing you can do to improve your emotional health and wellbeing is to control the information that goes into your mind. In other words, avoid input that causes you anxiety or distress as much as possible. An excellent example of this is watching the news. Unfortunately, most men associate watching the news with keeping in touch with the world around them. The truth of the matter is that most news channels focus on sensational stories, often embellishing them to increase the "wow factor." This means that rather than staying on top of current affairs, you are simply subjecting yourself to stressful, frustrating stories that are designed to elicit an emotional response. The solution is to avoid watching the news every single day, choosing instead to limit your exposure to once or twice a week. Furthermore, be selective on the sources you use to get your information. Choose sources that stick to the facts rather than opinions that are aimed at getting you emotionally charged.

The other side of the coin is that of seeking out things that provide positive emotional responses. In other words, do things that make you happy. If watching sporting events makes you happy, then do that. In fact, rather than settling for watching your favorite team on TV, take the time and effort to buy season tickets to watch them play in the flesh. This will take the experience to a whole new level, one that provides you and your loved ones the best results possible. If sporting events aren't your thing, but going to the movies, hobbies, gardening, fishing, or any other similar activity is what works then do that thing and do it well. Get the best gear, treat yourself to all the perks, spare no expense. After all, the more you invest in your happiness, the happier you will be.

Spiritual Self-Care

Finally, there is the aspect of spiritual self-care. This is another area where modern-day stereotypes serve to undermine a person's chances of true success. "Manly men" are supposed to be the self-reliant, grab-life-by-the-horns, conquer-the-world type of people who have little time for self-reflection and no need for contemplation. However, any true Alpha Male will attest to the fact that your values and beliefs are where you will find strength when you need it the most. This means that you need to take the time to develop and nurture your values and beliefs daily.

One way to achieve this goal is to find a practice that enables you to reflect on things. The things you reflect on can change from one day to the next, depending on circumstances. You might reflect on a particularly challenging situation at work for as long as it takes to resolve the issue. You might want to reflect on how to go about pursuing the girl or job of your dreams. There may be times when you do personal introspection, allowing you to contemplate who you are and where you are going. This will ensure that you always have a firm grasp on your life and that you avoid drifting aimlessly through life like countless people do every day.

Meditation is an easy and effective practice that can allow you to reflect or to clear your mind altogether if that is your choice. Numerous forms of meditation allow you to find the one that works best for you. Some are designed to release stress and anxiety, while others are more focused on clearing your mind and detaching from the outside world. Like physical exercise, you don't have to choose only one. Instead, you can mix it up and practice the form of meditation that best suits your needs at any particular moment. It only takes ten to fifteen minutes a day to meditate, meaning you can incorporate the practice into your daily routine without any problems at all.

Chapter 16: Setting Alpha Male Goals

So far, this book has provided all of the tools, insights, and directions you need to begin transforming your life into that of a true Alpha Male. However, there is one more piece of the puzzle that needs to be put in place before the big picture can be realized. That piece is setting goals. The importance of setting goals simply cannot be overstated. While many believe that the reasons they are unable to turn their dreams into reality are a lack of resources, time, or energy, the simple truth is that most people fall short due to a lack of goals. Goals are what turn dreams into achievable tasks, actions that can be taken daily to reach the desired destination. In short, goals are what turn abstract, intangible dreams into quantifiable reality. Therefore, to change your life in any way, shape or form, you must begin by setting the necessary goals. This chapter will discuss the nature of goals, as well as effective ways to set reasonable and achievable goals, thereby giving you the final element needed for creating the lifestyle of an Alpha Male.

What Exactly Is A Goal?

Many people mistakenly associate dreams with goals. Therefore, if you want to be rich, you might say your goal is to be rich. Unfortunately, this isn't entirely accurate. It would be more correct to say that your dream is to be rich. The goal is the step or set of steps in the plan that will lead you to that outcome. Knowing the destination is just the first step; it is the step of knowing your dream.

The next step is deciding how you will get there. You probably need to plot your journey. You may have to stop once or twice, depending on how far you have to go. How long it will take, which paths to choose, and whether you need to stop along the way are all part of planning the journey. This is the act of setting goals. Each path you enter is a goal, and each stop is a goal; every element of the journey, including when you leave, and when you return, are all goals. They are measurable actions that will lead you to your dream.

This is where most people fall short. By mistaking the dream for a goal, they never take the time to plot the course that will take them to where they want to be. They usually never even take the first step, since they are unsure as to which step to take. When you have your course plotted, you know where to go and when to go, allowing you to effectively take the actions needed to achieve your dream.

Methods for Effective Goal Setting

As with anything else in life, simply setting goals isn't always enough. Instead, you need to set the right goals in the right way. This will make all the difference when it comes to actually achieving the goals you set. Fortunately, there is a simple formula for effective goal setting, known as the SMARTER goal system, and it works like this:

- **S**pecific: Make sure always to set specific goals. Instead of saying you want to lose weight, set the goal of reaching a target weight, such as one hundred and eighty pounds. This is a specific goal in which you can easily track your progress.

- **M**easurable: The next step is to set a measurable goal. In the case of reaching a target weight, you need to measure where that weight is from where you currently are. Thus, if you weigh two hundred pounds, then your measurable goal is to lose twenty pounds.

- Actionable: This is where you begin to plot your course with regard to achieving your overall goal. If you want to lose twenty pounds, you can set actions such as eating healthier foods or exercising more regularly. This turns the goal from an ambition into an achievable action.

- Realistic: Sometimes, people make the mistake of setting goals that are too large to achieve. In the case of losing twenty pounds, you might choose to break the goal down into four smaller goals of losing five pounds per week. This takes the stress out of an "all or nothing" scenario, giving you easier targets to reach.

- Time-bound: This part of goal setting has two elements. The first element is when you start. If you want to lose weight, decide on when you will start taking action. The next element is the deadline. This is when you hope to achieve your goal. Thus, your goal should now be to lose five pounds in one week, starting tomorrow.

- Evaluate: When you have your measurable goal and your timeframe, you can begin evaluating your progress. If you have only lost one pound halfway through your seven-day deadline, then you can look at either increasing your efforts, perhaps by engaging in more exercise or eating better, or extending the deadline. In the end, it's always better to alter the goal than to give up on it altogether.

- Reward: The final phase of goal setting is to reward yourself for the progress you make. For example, each time you lose five pounds, you can choose to reward yourself by purchasing that DVD you have wanted for awhile, or some other relatively inexpensive item that acts as an incentive. Not only will this encourage you to keep going, but it will also program your mind to crave achieving the goals you set. When you achieve the big goal, you can go clothes shopping as a reward, treating yourself to a new wardrobe that will show off your new look.

Setting SMARTER goals increases your chances of achieving those goals, and that will change your life in a couple of very significant ways. First, your self-confidence will grow stronger and stronger with every goal you achieve. Therefore, as you achieve more goals, you will grow in confidence, giving you the courage to chase more and larger goals. The second way that this will change your life is that it will increase your success overall. Each goal will improve your life in some way. Therefore, as you accomplish more goals, you will be eager to set even more goals, which will improve your life exponentially, enabling you to create the life of your dreams.

Specific Goals for The Alpha Male

Now that you know the importance of goals and how to go about setting them, the final step is to set goals that are specific for an Alpha Male. The following are some goals that will help you to develop the Alpha Male lifestyle you both desire and deserve:

- **Improve your Image:** As we discussed, this takes many forms, including the clothes you wear, your physique, and even your grooming habits. Therefore, you must break this overall goal down into smaller, more manageable goals. The first will be to improve your hairstyle. Give yourself thirty days to find a stylist who will help you to achieve the look that is right for you. Next, you will want to work on getting your weight to an ideal level. Give yourself thirty days to achieve a specific weight (if that is a goal that is achievable in this timeframe). Finally, you will want to improve your wardrobe. Give yourself another thirty days to change your clothing style, giving you the Alpha Male look that will attract all the right attention. Make this your last step, as you will want to be at your right weight and have a hairstyle ready to define which clothes work best for you.

- **Improve your Self-Image:** This is another goal that will have many aspects. One aspect is that of establishing your values. Take a week or two to carefully contemplate those things that truly define who you are and the life you want to live. Once you have chosen your values, you need to integrate them into your day to day life in the form of the choices you make and the actions you perform. Next, increase your positivity. Begin spending time around positive people, feeding off of their energy, and using them as inspiration for chasing your dreams. Finally, take thirty days to work on developing your charm. The more charming you act, the more charming you will feel. This will increase your self-esteem as well as your self-confidence when interacting with other people.

- **Chase your Dreams:** Once you have improved yourself inside and out, it is time to start turning your dreams into reality. Take some time to decide what you want to achieve. If it is winning the perfect woman, landing the perfect job, or achieving some other life-changing ambition, make that your purpose. Once you have chosen your purpose, start setting goals on how to reach that destination. Give yourself thirty days to come up with a destination and a solid plan on how to reach that destination. Use the SMARTER method to break your overall goal into smaller, more achievable goals that can be measured and tracked effectively. Now that you have developed the heart, mind, and appearance of a true Alpha Male, there is no dream beyond your reach. Now you can start creating the life you have always wanted, the life of your dreams.

Conclusion

Now that you have read this book, you have all the insights and tools you need to begin your journey toward becoming an Alpha Male. From identifying and overcoming those elements that have robbed you of self-esteem to developing the habits needed to increase your overall sense of self-worth, you can now transform your self-esteem into the vibrant and robust one only found in an Alpha Male. Furthermore, by following the proven techniques provided, you can form the habits that will increase your self-confidence, thereby giving you the drive and ambition needed to pursue and achieve your goals. Finally, you now have the methods and techniques needed to establish clear and achievable goals, the sort that will enable you to turn your dreams into reality by giving you the ability to pursue those dreams in a realistic and meaningful way. Whether you dream of landing the perfect job, of attracting the perfect wife, or of living a life that makes you stand out from the rest, you now have everything you need to make those dreams come true. The very best of luck on your journey to becoming an Alpha Male and creating the successful life you both desire and deserve!

Sources

https://themighty.com/2018/10/low-self-esteem-habits/

https://www.telegraph.co.uk/health-fitness/living-with-erectile-dysfunction/why-men-lack-confidence/

https://guycounseling.com/men-destroy-self-esteem/

https://conqueryourconfidence.com/10-signs-of-low-self-esteem-in-men-how-to-overcome-insecurities/

https://brightside.me/wonder-people/10-secret-fears-90-of-men-never-talk-about-386910/

https://goodmenproject.com/guy-talk/signs-of-an-insecure-man-cmtt/

https://goodmenproject.com/featured-content/19-men-reveal-what-their-biggest-insecurities-are-when-it-comes-to-dating/

https://www.youtube.com/watch?v=ZCvle-Loc50

https://www.devex.com/news/how-self-doubt-manifests-in-men-versus-women-92506,

https://www.realmenrealstyle.com/overcome-self-doubt/

https://conqueryourconfidence.com/10-signs-of-low-self-esteem-in-men-how-to-overcome-insecurities/

https://www.youtube.com/watch?v=beg57qXMZTE

https://www.psychologytoday.com/us/blog/mind-your-body/201810/positive-body-image-in-men,

https://www.mirror-mirror.org/body-image-men.htm

https://www.huffingtonpost.co.uk/jessica-lovejoy/body-image-issues-in-men_b_5514957.html?

https://www.intechopen.com/books/weight-loss/men-s-body-image-the-effects-of-an-unhealthy-body-image-on-psychological-behavioral-and-cognitive-he

https://goodmenproject.com/featured-content/5-life-changing-habits-that-build-self-esteem-cmtt/

https://www.irreverentgent.com/self-confidence-for-men/

https://www.youtube.com/watch?v=s2aFCuzeab4

https://www.youtube.com/watch?v=SAXwtyl0MEs

https://www.youtube.com/watch?v=yMCHgxLyoRQ

https://www.youtube.com/watch?v=2c4Jz41IZmk,

https://understandingrelationships.com/women-prefer-alpha-males/35905,

https://www.youtube.com/watch?v=kFSAe7X8Nls

https://www.knowledgeformen.com/how-to-be-an-alpha-male/

https://www.youtube.com/watch?v=vFg20vvN5H4

https://www.youtube.com/watch?v=PzB92OQzKG4

http://chadhowsefitness.com/2012/10/stop-being-a-pussy-persist/

https://heartiste.org/2012/12/17/persistence-the-underrated-alpha-male-quality/

https://www.youtube.com/watch?v=QGvmAhcNRuU

https://www.youtube.com/watch?v=O7xuL7gAM5w

https://therationalmale.com/2011/10/12/frame/

http://oldschool-calisthenic.ro/alpha-male-look/

https://brobible.com/sports/article/building-alpha-male-physique/

https://www.youtube.com/watch?v=4fcxxeefmTk

https://www.youtube.com/watch?v=dqXZYDGORos

https://themaaximumlife.com/mental-toughness-is-the-key-to-becoming-a-manly-man/

https://theartofcharm.com/confidence/become-alpha-male-staying-gentleman/

https://get-a-wingman.com/alpha-male-body-language-hacks-that-instantly-boost-your-attractiveness/

https://www.youtube.com/watch?v=TPSsLb8HNoE

https://www.guysplaybook.com/alpha-males-have-clear-purpose/
https://www.artofmanliness.com/articles/30-days-to-a-better-man-day-1-define-your-core-values/
https://www.vibe.com/2019/06/masculinity-and-self-care-feature
https://goodmenproject.com/featured-content/7-better-self-care-tips-for-guys-wcz/
https://www.youtube.com/watch?v=kSVqu9uK1hw,
https://www.youtube.com/watch?v=XpKvs-apvOs,
https://productcoalition.com/how-to-hack-goal-setting-for-more-confidence-31ecdaa4deea, https://www.knowledgeformen.com/goal-setting/
https://www.thebabereport.com/6-reasons-why-women-love-dating-direct-men/
https://www.irreverentgent.com/how-to-look-more-handsome-and-attractive/
https://www.glidedesign.com/12-examples-of-persistence-paying-off/

Check out another book by Kory Heaton

www.ingramcontent.com/pod-product-compliance
Lightning Source LLC
Chambersburg PA
CBHW051736290426
43661CB00124B/779